Redesigning Library Services

A MANIFESTO

Michael Buckland

Foreword by
Michael Gorman

AMERICAN LIBRARY ASSOCIATION
Chicago and London | 1992

Cover and text designed by
Harriett Banner

Composed by Publishing Services, Inc.
in Schneidler and Triumvirate on Xyvision/Cg8600.

Printed on 50-pound Glatfelter, a PH-neutral
stock, and bound in 10-point C1S cover stock
by Malloy Lithographing, Inc.

The paper used in this publication meets the minimum requirements
of American National Standard for Information Sciences—
Permanence of Paper for Printed Library Materials, ANSI Z39.48-1984.
∞

Library of Congress Cataloging-in-Publication Data

Buckland, Michael Keeble.
    Redesigning library services : a manifesto / Michael Buckland.
       p.   cm.
    Includes bibliographical references.
    ISBN 0-8389-0590-0
    1. Library science—Technological innovations—Management.
2. Information technology—Management. 3. Libraries—Automation—
Management. 4. Library administration. 5. Libraries and readers.
6. Organizational change. I. Title.
Z678.9.B82 1992   92-10546
025.5'24—dc20   CIP

Printed in the United States of America.

96 95 94 93 92   5 4 3 2 1

Contents

Figures

Foreword

There have been a number of books on the future of libraries and librarianship. Some would say that far too many such books have been published. This is because the bulk of these books are unrealistically futuristic or technically obsessed or consist of lengthy and arid speculations on the future of higher education, the publishing industry, and the other contexts within which we work. Michael Buckland's book falls into none of these categories. It is both visionary and practical. There is knowledge and information in this book that is of immediate use to librarians, administrators of libraries of all kinds, university administrators, faculty, boards of trustees, and all others interested in the future of library service. It is in this utility, and in the fact that this book is pitched in the medium term, that its strengths and value can be found.

One of the most telling points made by the author is that, like it or not, libraries will have to deal with the provision of access to electronic documents. He rightly and shrewdly avoids arguments about the exact proportion of such documents compared with the more familiar linear documents of yesterday and today. This is pragmatism at its best. *Que sera, sera*, and it behooves all of us to plan for what we know will happen before we plan for what might happen. It seems most likely that the library will be dealing with documents of all kinds for the foreseeable future and, probably, indefinitely. The mix will be different and the library of the future may look different, but, as Michael Buckland points out, librarianship has enduring values and enduring ends. The wisdom of the assessment of the future found in this book is that it keeps those values and ends firmly in sight, while regarding as sacred none of the means that we use and have used to achieve them.

It is very easy to accept the familiar without question. It is also easy to assume that the predicted future will remedy the failings of the past and present. Michael Buckland does neither of these things. His analysis of the "Paper Library" (the library of linear documents controlled by paper files) and the "Automated Library" (the library of linear documents controlled by electronic files) is deceptively simple, as are all worthwhile insights. In reading the sections of this book devoted to these topics, one can see very clearly where we have been, where we are, and where we may be going. His analysis is a penetrating light shone on the familiar that shows those with eyes to see that unquestioned assumptions are dangerously misleading. When the libraries of yesterday and today are contrasted with the hypothetical library of tomorrow—the Electronic Library—one does not have to agree with every jot and tittle of the author's analysis to realize how important it is to define the destination *before* one equips oneself for the journey.

Buckland's Electronic Library is defined as one ". . . in which documents are stored and can be used in electronic (or similarly machine readable) form." There are two important aspects of this definition. Note that the documents are *stored* and *can be used* in electronic form. First, the fact that they are so stored does not preclude them being printed for use as a conventional text. At present, the prevalence of such printing is making a mockery of the "paperless society" predictions that were so popular a decade ago. It is entirely possible that the Electronic Library will contain not only electronic and linear (mainly printed) documents but also a hybrid of the two in which the library acts as a kind of publisher-cum-bookseller providing high quality printings of electronic texts or graphics. This would, of course, have a revolutionary effect on the role of libraries and the nature of the publishing and bookselling trades. The second important implication of the definition of the Electronic Library is in the fact that the documents can be used in electronic form. The use of digital electronic documents can go well beyond that of simply reading a text or seeing an image. This flexibility (conferred by the ability to edit, merge, add to, make subsets of, rearrange, etc., electronic documents) will have profound, and not invariably benign, effects on libraries, library users, and library service. These are important matters and everyone involved with libraries should be considering them.

Another cardinal virtue of this book can be found in its emphasis on service to library users. Libraries are, essentially, utilitarian constructs. That which tends toward the greatest happiness of the greatest number is good; that which does not is bad. Libraries exist to serve and to be used. Michael Buckland clearly shows us the way to increase the service that libraries can deliver and to understand the likely demands of the library user of the future. One of the sad consequences of the confusion between means and ends that has been endemic in librarianship is that too many have lost sight of the simple purpose of libraries—to serve as many people as well as we can. Libraries, their collections, and technological advance are not good in themselves. They are means to vital ends—disseminating knowledge and information; preserving the records of culture and civilization; and raising and maintaining the quality of intellectual and social life. It is a considerable achievement to have not only provided a cogent analysis of the past, present, and likely future of libraries but also to have used that analysis to point the way to the practical consequences of change. The author has done all this, too, in a brief compass.

The best books provide us with insights into, and new ways of looking at, things and ideas. This is sometimes called the shock of recognition. *Redesigning Library Services* is such a book. More, it provides us with the ways in which we can use those insights to do practical things that will improve libraries and library service. In essence, what the author is telling us is

here is where we are and where we have been;
here is the likely direction in which we are going;
here is the impact of the likely future on libraries, library service, and library users; and,
here is how we should organize ourselves and run our libraries to respond to the challenges of change.

This is a useful book because it is practical and an important book because it will color the way in which we see libraries. It is a wonderful antidote to the nihilism that has been induced in some by technological change. It affirms the importance of libraries and shows us how we can have faith in the future of libraries without taking refuge in nostalgia. It is, in the very best sense of the terms, progressive and forward-looking.

Michael Gorman
Dean of Library Services
California State University, Fresno

Preface

The future of library services arouses both excitement and unease. With the coming of on-line library catalogs, technical changes that have been taking place in the back rooms of libraries for several years suddenly become much more apparent to everyone. The on-line library catalog is probably the most sophisticated computer system of any type in routine, direct use by the general public. Some kind of dramatic change in library service is already afoot. On-line bibliographic (and other) databases have been available for several years and, as personal computers and telecommunications have become so much more widespread, the idea of "electronic libraries" becomes less implausible. There are sweeping assertions about an emerging "information society" and reports of complex maneuverings within an "information industry" that includes computer firms, phone companies, publishers, "information providers," and diverse others. Meanwhile there is clear evidence that public, school, and university libraries are in some distress as public sector undertakings with substantial appetites for book funds, new buildings, staff, and, now, new technology, in circumstances of severe budgetary constraint.

There is, of course, a massive, specialized literature on library technology, but it is primarily concerned with how to make things work now (or soon) and is of little direct benefit to those who should be worrying about how library services might or should evolve over the next ten years.

Consider the public library trustee, the faculty library committee member, or the librarian charged with developing a strategic plan for a library's development or facing the major investment that a new library building would require. What could be said that might explain how library services have been changing and how they seem likely to change in the future? What could be provided as background reading and as a basis for discussion? There is a gap between the technical details of today's computer problems and blue-sky predictions of distant electronic information futures. What might help fill that gap? What might be said that could be relevant to strategic planning in, say, the five- to ten-year range?

Any attempt to explain the past and to predict change is foolhardy. In this case the importance of the issues seemed worth the effort and the risk. If the account presented here does no more than to provoke better accounts by others, we would all benefit. This book draws on years as a user of several libraries, some years as a librarian, and other years as an educator of future librarians. However, it derives most directly from a close involvement in discussions concerning the plans, policies, and long-term future development of the libraries of the nine campuses of the University of California during 1983 to 1987 and from subsequent reflection on the issues that emerged.

Technological change is only one influence on institutions. There are also cultural changes, changes in political and social values, economic changes, and changes in what is known and understood. The discussion in this book concentrates on the long-term effects of technological change on library services because they are significant and because they appear to be more predictable than changes from other causes. Bits and pieces of what is predicted here do not require a crystal ball as they are already happening.

I have benefited greatly from the ideas and help of many people, especially Edwin B. Brownrigg, Michael Gorman, Rolf Høyer, Gary S. Lawrence, Clifford A. Lynch, Stephen R. Salmon, and Raynard C. Swank, but they should not be blamed for deficiencies in what follows.

Introduction

PURPOSE OF LIBRARIES

The central purpose of libraries is to provide a service: access to information.

The good news is that additional, different means for providing library service are becoming available in a manner unprecedented since the nineteenth century. The challenge for all concerned with libraries is to determine how, whether, and when these new means should be used.

Libraries exist for the benefit of the mind, but they have serious practical problems coping with the acquisition, storage, and handling of the documents and records with which they deal. Major constraints arise from the technology used as a means for providing service. Any change in technology that would have a significant effect on the methods available for acquisition, storage, delivery, or searching procedures could have important consequences for library service. Consequently, a continuing quest for technological improvement has been and should continue to be important.

Those responsible for providing library service have been more or less conscious of the nature of the underlying problems to be solved, and some of the more gifted and farsighted groped toward radical solutions based on a deep understanding of the nature of the problems. The key elements of the probable form of the electronic library of the twenty-first century were being glimpsed, albeit imperfectly, by the early 1930s by perceptive thinkers. More recently, visions of the library of the future have been associated with speculation on the demise of the book, the supposed obsolescence of librarians, and other questionable rhetoric.

Discussion of providing "access" to "information" is commonly incomplete or misleading. The term "information" is used with very differing meanings and is commonly used attributively to refer to books, journals, databases, and other physical objects regarded as potentially informative. Access to a potentially informative document depends on identifying, locating, and having affordable physical access to it. However, for someone to become informed, to become more knowledgeable, requires more: The reader needs to be able to understand and evaluate what is in it. If what is found is rejected or not understood, then little informing will have been achieved.

Much has been written in recent years on the possible impact of new technology on "the library of the future." This is nothing new. It could be that long-term visions have a beneficial effect in stimulating debate and thought. However, one may suspect that little of the rhetoric and few of the specific technological proposals have been of much direct help to those with the heavy responsibility of planning for the future of any particular library: the administrators, funders, librarians, and library users developing five- or ten-year plans, contemplating the high cost of a major new library building, or worrying about the relationship between the familiar technology of paper and the less familiar, unstable technology of computers. The problems of existing libraries are severe. Visions of electronic libraries seem uncertain and suspect. Even if such a vision seems good, it is not at all clear that plausible paths of development from here to there have been adequately mapped.

Redesigning Library Services has been written on three assumptions:

1. There has been insufficient attention to *strategic* planning, that is, the making of decisions relative to a three- to ten-year time frame. We seek to examine the middle ground between the large literature on possible options among the tactical and operational decisions made day-to-day and month-by-month and the sweeping visions of endless, interlinked electronic villages. The latter offer little continuity with present experience and can make those who are dependent on existing services understandably nervous. Some people are enthusiasts for electronic solutions; others want to avoid the high cost of continuing present operations.

2. A disproportionate amount of attention has been paid to new information technology. It is not really that too much attention has been given to it, but rather that not enough critical attention has been given to the characteristics of the familiar technology of paper. We adapt to what we adopt. What is familiar tends to be transparent. It may take some conscious effort to appraise critically and evaluatively what we are so accustomed to.

3. There is, in fact, considerable experience on which our strategic planning can be based, more than is generally realized.

Suppose that one were charged with making recommendations concerning the development of a library service over a three- to ten-year range, what sort of conclusions might one be justified in reaching? The purpose of this book is to suggest some general bases for planning or, at least, to provide a general framework for thinking about future library services. (Advice on procedural details for handling specific planning activities can be found in numerous management texts.)

The purpose being pursued in library service is the provision of access to books, journals, and other informative materials. Libraries have never had a monopoly since much of what is in demand is also available in personal collections and bookshops, from personal contacts, and, indeed, from other sorts of libraries. However, even if it is not a monopoly, it is clearly the major role and niche of library service. Now, in addition to the customary difficulties in providing library service, the radical changes in the technology available as *means* for providing service leaves the future unclear.

In such a situation we need to be prepared to retreat to first principles, to reaffirm or redefine the mission and the role of a library. Library service is a busy, service-oriented activity, with a deeply rooted emphasis, reflected in the professional literature, on practical and technical matters, on means, rather than on ends, and on tactics rather than strategy. There is so much more written, for example, on how to build collections than on the roles that collections play. There is so much more on how to create catalogs than on how catalogs are used. Nevertheless, there is currently a healthy awareness that major changes are likely and a recognition, for example, of some convergence between library services, computing services, and telecommunications services, of probable changes in the publishing world, and that library management is, at least in part, concerned as much with the management of service as with the management of books.[1]

FOUNDATIONS OF LIBRARY SERVICE

Library services have two bases:

the role of library service is to facilitate access to documents; and
the mission of a library is to support the mission of the institution or
the interests of the population served.

Interpreting these two general statements for any given situation provides the foundations for effective library service.

The first statement stimulates us to ask how "facilitate," "access," and "documents" should be interpreted and how the role of the library service is related to the roles of the book trade, computing, and other services. Hitherto the dominant interpretation has been the judicious assembling of local collections as the only effective means of providing convenient physical access to documents, augmented by bibliographic tools and advice.

The second general statement entails that the determination of what should be done is unique to each specific context.

Examining strategies for the development of library services requires that three conditions be met.

1. We need to distinguish between means and ends. The *purposes of* and *justification for* library service should not be confused with the techniques and technologies adopted as *means* for providing service, even though our options are limited by the available techniques and technologies.

The long period of relative stability from the late nineteenth century up to the 1970s in the means for providing library service is just the kind of situation in which it becomes easy for the distinction between ends and means to become blurred. So long as there is but one principal means to an end (even with variations in details and in scale), more of the *end* is achieved by more of the *means* and the distinction between ends and means has little significance in practice. But this blurring of the distinction hinders dealing effectively with *alternative means* if and when—as now—they become available.

The advent of novel, alternative means for service increases the need to think clearly about the ends of library service. The ends may not change very much, but they are likely to need to be reinterpreted and reaffirmed at intervals in a changing world. In any case, responsible selection of means depends on prior selection of ends.

2. Alternative means do need to be explored aggressively otherwise the options will not be known. With that we need to distinguish between tactical (short-term) measures and strategic (long-term) measures.

3. Discussion both of means and of ends implies consideration not only of what is good and what is not so good, but also of different sorts of goodness.

"How good is it?" is a measure of quality or, in effect, a measure of capability with respect to serving some actual or imagined demand. This kind of goodness is appropriate for the evaluation and measurement of means, of tools and techniques for providing service, as in "a good collection" or "a good catalog." Output or performance measures are commonly of this type.

"What good does it do?" is a different kind of question, appropriate to the evaluation of ends and to the relating of means to ends. What sort of good do we most want to achieve within available resources? Planning processes that concern themselves with *which* performance measures to use are of this type.

Another form of goodness lies in the question "How well is it done?", which has to do with cost-effectiveness, efficiency, and effective management generally.[2]

THREE TYPES OF LIBRARY

Modern library service as we know it was largely developed in the second half of the nineteenth century, characterized by:

1. The idea of library collections being for service;
2. The notion of systematic, purposeful book selection;
3. The adoption of a series of technical innovations, such as relative shelf location (shelving books relative to each other rather than on specific shelves), improved cataloging codes, more systematic approaches to shelf arrangement and subject classification, card catalogs, and sustained efforts at standardization and cooperation; and,
4. In the twentieth century, a trend toward self-service, with open stacks and public catalogs.

Terminology has evolved, the scale of operation is much increased, and technical refinements have been made. Nevertheless examination of early issues of *College and Research Libraries* of fifty years ago, and of the *Library Journal* another fifty years before that, shows that many of their underlying concerns are still strikingly contemporary. The following three types of library provision, based on the technology used, provide a convenient framework for discussing future library service.

Until recently the technical operations of libraries (e.g., purchasing, processing, cataloging, and circulation) and library materials (primarily texts) were both based on paper and cardboard: We call this the "Paper Library." Strictly speaking, libraries have always included materials other than paper, such as clay tablets, vellum, film, and so on, but these other media make little difference for our present purposes.

Over the past two decades, the technical operations of libraries have become based on computer technology while library materials still remain overwhelmingly on paper and paper-like media: the "Automated Library."

As of 1992, the increase in the amount and the variety of material becoming available in electronic form is quite dramatic: government statistics, medieval texts, satellite images, images of museum objects, all kinds of interesting things. The prospect that library *materials*, as well as library operations, will increasingly be in electronic form indicates a further change in the means of library service: the "Electronic Library." See table 1 below.

The concept of the Electronic Library is important because library *materials* will increasingly be available in machine-readable form, users will need access to them, and *access will, therefore, have to be provided*. One can speculate about the eventual balance between paper materials and electronic materials or, if one wishes, on the prospects for paperless libraries, but these issues are of little significance compared with the underlying assumption that arrangements for access to some materials in electronic form will have to be provided. Today libraries are, or are becoming, Automated Libraries, with the imminent prospect of needing to evolve, at least in part, into Electronic Libraries. Since paper documents (and other nonelectronic media such as film) seem unlikely to disappear, we may expect the Automated Library and the Electronic Library to coexist indefinitely. More specifically, we can expect, and should plan for, any real library service to be a blend: part Automated Library and part Electronic Library.

The shift to computer-based technical operations and, more especially, the advent of library materials in electronic form indicate the prospect of radical changes in the *means* of library service. Library materials in electronic form differ significantly from traditional media. In particular, unlike paper and microform, it is possible to make electronic media available so that they

can be used from a distance,
can be used by more than one person at a time, and
can be used in more different ways.

The significance of these three differences is profound and will be examined in some detail.

Table 1. Technological Bases of Library Operations and Materials

	Technical Operations	*Library Materials*
Paper Library	Paper	Paper
Automated Library	Computer	Paper
Electronic Library	Computer	Electronic media

LIBRARY USERS

How are the circumstances of library users changing? Part of the answer is that some of those whom the libraries are funded to serve are themselves adopting electronic habits, making increasing use of the new information technology of computers, electronic storage, and telecommunications in addition to the old information technology of pen, paper, and photocopier. The new electronic tools provide powerful options for working with data, text, sound, and images. As examples, consider the reduction in labor now required for producing revised documents, for complex calculations, for image enhancement, and for the statistical analysis of large sets of data and passages of text.

Library services have to do with support for learning, both the study of what others have discovered and research to discover what is apparently not yet known. Yet the librarian's role is often very indirect. The librarian's concern, rather than being with knowledge itself, is usually with *representations* of knowledge—with texts and images. Further, much of the time, the concern is not really with the texts themselves, but with text-bearing objects: the millions of books, journals, photographs, and databases that fill our libraries' shelves. Librarians generally assist, not by giving answers directly, but by referring the inquirer to a book. Somehow we need to maintain the underlying concern with how individuals acquire knowledge. Librarians must concern themselves with how individuals use information (books, journals, etc.) and also with how they become informed and knowledgeable.

The old information technology of pen, paper, and, latterly, photocopier did not encourage much departure from library use as "read, think, write." In contrast—for some—the new information technology is transforming the use of library materials, with computer-based techniques for identifying, locating, accessing, transferring, analyzing, manipulating, comparing, and revising texts, images, and data, derived in part from the library's electronic resources. A wholly new dimension of the use of library services is emerging. What would do more for users, for the development of library service, and for rapport with users than providing assistance that keeps pace with these changes?

OUTLINE

In the next chapter, we review some characteristics of the Paper Library, its strengths, weaknesses, and persistent attempts to remedy or compensate for the inherent limitations of the technology of paper. Then, we briefly summarize the Automated Library and our experience with it in Chapter 3.

Alongside the development of the Automated Library has been the parallel development of computer-based bibliographies. In Chapter 4, we explore some of the significant implications of the automation of bibliographies and of libraries' technical operations.

The rise of electronic documents and the nature of the Electronic Library are outlined in Chapter 5. We consider some of the consequences of the rise of the Electronic Library for collection development in Chapter 6.

In Chapter 7 we consider the needs and changing environment of library users. Chapter 8 touches upon some management considerations. The final chapter, Chapter 9, provides a summary and some conclusions.

It seems that the relative stability of the past century is but a prologue to another period of radical change, comparable in significance to that of the late nineteenth century with its exciting renaissance of ideas and techniques. This time change is enabled less by new ideas than by a shift in the underlying technology, which is all the more reason to reassess our assumptions about the future of libraries. As operations and services become more complex and more capital-intensive, ad hoc, unsystematic decision making can lead library services down unproductive paths. Correcting mistakes becomes expensive and disruptive.

Creative planning is of central importance because of the superiority of planning over merely reacting to events. We—funders, providers, and users of library services—need to reflect creatively on what we do and why. Planning offers us a chance to create the future.

Notes

1. Raymond K. Neff, "Merging Libraries and Computer Centers: Manifest Destiny or Manifestly Deranged," *EDUCOM Bulletin* 20 (Winter 1985):8–12, 16.

2. On library goodness see Richard M. Orr, "Measuring the Goodness of Library Services: A General Framework for Considering Quantitative Measures," *Journal of Documentation* 29 (Sept. 1973):315–32; Michael K. Buckland, "Concepts of Library Goodness," *Canadian Library Journal* 39 (Apr. 1982):63–66.

2

The Paper Library

The Paper Library has problems associated with it that need to be set forth in order to provide a basis for a balanced view of the Automated Library and of the Electronic Library and for a clearer appreciation of the contrasting capabilities of the Paper Library, the Automated Library, and the Electronic Library.

PAPER TECHNOLOGY

Paper is an instance of a traditional, "hard-copy" medium. Strictly, paper is not the only traditional medium in libraries, but, since other traditional media, such as vellum and microfilm, have characteristics that are substantially the same, we can, for our present purposes, subsume them under paper. We use paper as the predominant example of and symbol for hard-copy media in general.

Library services as we know them best are based on the technology of paper. Card, as in card catalogs, is but a stiff form of paper. Libraries' technical operations are steadily being computerized and, thereby, Paper Libraries are now being transformed into what we are calling Automated Libraries. The Paper Library proved effective and durable for an extended period. Nevertheless, the problems inherent in the Paper Library are real and substantial. Through sheer familiarity, we may cease to be conscious of the constraints of what we regard as normal. People worry, as they should, about the advantages and disadvantages of using computers, but the advantages and disadvantages of using paper, which is thoroughly familiar, get little attention. The serious limitation of paper needs to be reviewed explicitly if we are to make an informed and balanced appraisal of the other options, the Automated Library and the Electronic Library.[1]

1. Paper is a strictly localized medium. It and the user must be the same place at the same time. A copy elsewhere cannot be used. It or a copy must be in the same place as the would-be reader. This may sound foolishly simple, but it has enormous practical consequences and dominates the design and operation of the Paper Library, the traditional library.

2. A single paper document can, in general, only be used by one person at a time.

3. Paper copies of paper documents can be made by reprinting and by photographic and more modern reprographic means, but the same limitations apply to a copy as to the original. It is as much a localized document as the original. Facsimile transmission ("fax"), which is becoming popular for short documents, can provide a remedy, but only by getting away from paper and using the transmission of an electronic copy of the document as an intermediary between the paper original in one place and creation of a paper copy in some other place.

4. Paper as a medium is rather inflexible. Individual copies of a document can have annotations added to them and, with sufficient standardization, paper documents can be interfiled. But paper documents really do not lend themselves to being merged, divided, reformatted, and restored to earlier versions.

5. Collections on paper become bulky and create storage problems.

PROBLEMS OF THE PAPER LIBRARY

Local Nature of Paper Documents

Because paper is a strictly localized medium, a copy in the Vatican Library is of little immediate benefit to a would-be reader in Hong Kong. It follows from this limitation that, in principle, there ought to be a copy of every needed document in every local collection where it is going to be needed and that copy should have been collected and processed for use before it is needed. Stated differently, every individual library collection ought, in theory, to include a copy of every document that its users will want. It is the localized nature of paper that makes us want our library to be conveniently local and our (and every other) library to contain a collection of materials that is not only skillfully selected but is also as large as can be afforded.

The localness of paper documents remains an unsolved constraint. A consequence is that each library collection is more or less skillfully selected to match the needs of those using it, which is an advantage over finding oneself in a vast warehouse of indiscriminately assembled materials, whether paper or electronic.

Disadvantages of the collection development practices of the Paper Library are that all libraries are more or less duplicative, complete collections cannot be afforded, and libraries that aspire to completeness become prohibitively expensive.

Librarians and library users have long wished for rapidly available, inexpensive facsimiles. Television was promptly recognized, at least as early as 1925, as demonstrating the potential of electronic telecommunications for remote access to library materials. "But what a revolution for information retrieval and especially for libraries television can bring," exclaimed the German librarian Walter Schürmeyer in 1935. "Perhaps one day we will see our reading rooms deserted and in their place a room without people in which books requested by telephone are displayed, which the users read in their homes using television."[2]

Space for Paper Documents

The sheer bulk of the Paper Library remains a major problem. The amount to be stored increases relentlessly. What library is not chronically short of space for its paper documents? Even in the U.S. library-building boom of 1967 to 1974, construction was not keeping pace with the amount of space needed to house the reported increases in the number of volumes held.[3] In California, the cost of constructing and equipping conventional academic library space is approaching $20 per volume. That the University of California needs twelve miles of additional shelving every year to house the growing paper collections of the nine campuses is a significant problem.

Books can be stored more compactly than on standard, open-access shelving that supports around 12.5 volumes per square foot of floor space. Unfortunately, compact storage techniques, such as denser forms of shelving or relegation to remoter, cheaper space, reduce the accessibility to the books which is the primary purpose of a library service.

Microphotography developed almost as early as photography itself, and its potential as a compact alternative to paper was soon recognized. Microphotography also offered a solution to another serious technological constraint of paper technology: the making of copies. Microfilm achieves both compactness and easy reproduction. These virtues were noticed by those who worried about the deficiencies of the Paper Library. The Belgian documentalist Paul Otlet, for example, proposed the use of standardized microfiche in 1906. He saw microforms not as a replacement for the book, but rather an expansion of the paper book into a new and more versatile form. In 1925, Otlet and the Belgian inventor Robert Goldschmidt described an easily manufactured "microphotographic library." It was composed of versatile "pocket-sized" viewing equipment and a portable cabinet one meter wide, one meter high, and about ten centimeters deep holding, on microfilm, 18,750 volumes of 350 pages each, the equivalent of 468 meters of conventional library shelving.[4]

Flexibility of Paper Documents

A constraint of paper documents is their inflexibility. Microfilm is little help in this regard. Microfilm can be copied, but alteration of the text on it is even more difficult than altering text on paper.

Paul Otlet anticipated the idea of hypertext, whereby texts are fragmented in smaller units (nodes) to be related to each other in complex and changing ways. Unfortunately, the dismembering and rearranging of paper documents, although feasible in principle, has severe limitations in practice, especially if one seeks to go beyond bibliographies and encyclopedia articles.

Catalogs in the Paper Library

The standard form of catalogs for most of the nineteenth century was in book form. Occasionally a small printed edition was produced to distribute knowledge of the library's holdings to users and to other libraries. But book-form catalogs are inflexible and inconvenient to update. One has to write in additions and deletions, insert new pages, respace existing entries, start separate supplements, and/or produce a new edition. Card catalogs as an innovation offered scope for the continuous and unlimited insertion, alteration, replacement, and removal of entries, but multiple copies of card catalogs are uneconomical and difficult to maintain.

Similarly, with any hard-copy form of catalog, each form of access requires a separate sequence: one card for the author, another card for the title, another card for each subject heading. Whether interfiled or in separate sequences, the bulk increases relentlessly. For access by call number an additional set of cards is required. The usefulness of a catalog could be greatly extended by providing separate "analytical" entries providing direct access to parts within books and journals, but many more cards would be needed. To search by date, which would sometimes be useful, would require yet another set of cards. The cost of the creation, housing, and, especially, maintenance of ever larger files increases steeply; so does the effort required to search in them. There is no technical reason not to have lots and lots of cards providing many different kinds of access in card catalogs, but the economic disincentives are persuasive.

During the first half of this century punched cards, edge-notched cards, and similar mechanical searching devices were developed for simple and Boolean selecting (i.e., searching for arbitrary combinations of index terms). However, they were not widely adopted for bibliographic purposes. Fritz Donker Duyvis, the Dutch documentalist, observed in 1931 that punched card equipment was simply inadequate for bibliographic searching and noted with foresight that a new type of equipment based on the type of digital circuitry then being developed for telephone systems was a more promising line of development for the sheer complexity of the Boolean and faceted subject-access techniques developed for bibliographic retrieval from the 1890s onward.[5]

Separation of Catalog from Text

In the Paper Library the catalog is physically quite separate from the text. One could find a book on the shelves but might be unable to find the entry for it in the catalog. Finding a catalog entry does not mean finding the book, merely a record of the official shelf location at which the book might or might not be at any given time. Card catalogs deal with ownership (actual or believed) as much as with the actual location of documents. The real solution is to develop an "integral" system in which the catalog entry and the text are somehow physically linked: Find one and you have found the other.

Having noted the dramatic saving of space that would result from using microform texts, the American librarian Fremont Rider asked in 1944 "Why might we not combine the micro-texts of our books, and the catalog cards for the same books, in one single entity? In other words, why could we not put our microbooks on the (at present entirely unused) backs of their own catalog cards?"[6] The argument was that if you had found the catalog card, you would have found the text, and the storage of the paper collections would become unnecessary. Rider foresaw dramatic reductions in acquisitions and space costs from the adoption of his proposed "micro-cards" combining catalog record and text. In a variation on this theme, chips of microfilm were sometimes mounted on index entries in punched and edge-notched cards ("aperture cards").[7]

Instead of adding the text to the catalog record one could add the catalog entry to the text, as was the case when index entries were added alongside the images of texts on a microfilm, much like the adding of a sound track to a movie. The use of photoelectric cells for searching microfilm for desired indexing terms and, thereby, the desired texts constituted an early form of electronic document retrieval designed by 1927 in Germany by Emanuel Goldberg. This technique was later enhanced and popularized by Vannevar Bush, Ralph Shaw, and others as the "microfilm rapid selector" and formed the technological basis of the imaginary "Memex" information machine.[8]

Separation of Users from Catalogs and Documents

For the Paper Library, the assembling of substantial, well-selected local collections is a necessary, but not sufficient, condition for effectiveness. *Local* means "near to users" but, as Robert T. Jordan stressed, there is in practice a significant difference between "near to users" and "where the users are."[9] Studies of the use of sources of information (libraries included) have invariably revealed that usage is in practice highly sensitive to physical accessibility: Usage falls off quite steeply even over quite small distances such as a few blocks in the case of a public library and the other side of campus for academic libraries. Jordan's 1970 book, *Tomorrow's Library,* is interesting as a poignant, pre-automation attempt to redress weaknesses inherent in technology of the Paper Library. With the Paper Library the user must make a journey to the library to consult the catalog and, short of a personal document delivery service, must visit the library to consult a document if it is, in fact, believed to be there.

Both the desire for proximity and the desire for reliable control fuel the popularity of departmental libraries in universities and neighborhood branches of public libraries. Administrators may worry that such decentralization is inefficient, wasteful, and an indulgence of users' inertia. But cost benefit (in contrast to cost minimization) depends heavily on the amount of use. User-friendliness in library service includes providing service to (or close to) wherever the intended users are.

Opening Hours

The Paper Library and the collections in the Automated Library need human beings to use them and to supervise them. Computers can be left unattended. Paper Libraries cannot. Even with extended hours, few Paper Libraries are open twenty-four hours a day, seven days a week. Most Paper Libraries are closed, allowing neither access nor service, most of the time.

Already in Use

Because only one person at a time can use a single paper document, there is always a chance that the document you want is being used by someone else at the time when you want it. The high cost of purchasing copies ahead of time, the difficulty of predicting demand, and the limited possibilities for making copies make this problem difficult to resolve. Further, because of the highly localized nature of paper and the limited opening hours, most libraries facilitate the use of paper documents by permitting them to be borrowed, commonly for weeks at a time. The effects of lending documents are intensified because the demand for documents in every library is highly skewed: Some books are more popular than others, and users tend to want the same documents. The combined effect of these features of the Paper Library is to reduce drastically the chances that the book you want will be available when you want it, even if the library is open. Study after study of academic libraries has indicated that the chance of finding a book that you want is around 60 percent, assuming that the library does own a copy. In other words, standard performance for a Paper Library is little better than a 50–50 chance that a document actually in the collection will be available when one looks for it.[10]

Time

As paper-based systems become larger and more complex, their use becomes more and more time-consuming. The physical separation of catalog from text and of user from both catalog and text increase. Distances to and within the library become greater. It may be necessary to wait to use what someone else is using. Reasons multiply why the elapsed time from initial impulse to completed use can be expected to be more and more protracted.

Scale

The problems of the Paper Library are in part a problem of scale. There are diseconomies of scale because unit costs of filing, finding, and reshelving increase as collections become larger.

PIONEERS

We have illustrated our account of the problems of paper libraries by mentioning some examples of pioneering attempts to use other forms of information technology to remedy the limitations of paper. Apart from rather simple uses of microforms and, for a while, punched cards, these proposals had little direct impact. They and their inventors have been largely forgotten. Yet it is noteworthy that the features currently assumed of the Electronic Library of the twenty-first century—compact storage, ease of reproduction, remote access to full text, hypertext, equipment capable of sophisticated searching in complex indexing systems, and other thoroughly contemporary notions—were foreseen at least in outline by practical idealists by 1935, before the invention of electronic digital computers.

The ideas of these innovative bibliographers, documentalists, and librarians are of interest for our purposes because they demonstrate that the significant weaknesses of the Paper Library were recognized, at least by the more perceptive observers. Further, they are encouraging because they indicate that steadfast attention to what is needed can provide a plausible basis for effective planning even before adequate new technology becomes a practical reality. If form should follow function, then concentration on the function should help us anticipate future forms.

Notes

1. Michael K. Buckland, "Library Materials: Paper, Microform, Database," *College and Research Libraries,* 49 (Mar. 1988):117–22.

2. Walter Schuermeyer, "Mitteilungen über einige technische Neuerungen und Anwendungsmethoden fotographischer Hilfegeräte für das dokumentarische Arbeiten" (Communications concerning some technical innovations and applications techniques for photographic tools for documentary work), *I.I.D. Communicationes* 3 (1) (1936):cols. Schü. 1–10. (Paper presented at the 13th Documentation Conference, Copenhagen, 1935).

3. For the space needs of the paper library see *Farewell to Alexandria: Solutions to Space, Growth, and Performance Problems of Libraries,* ed. Daniel Gore (Westport, Conn.: Greenwood Press, 1976). Within this book, the paper by Claudia Schnorrig, "Sizing Up the Space Problem in Academic Libraries" provides data for 1967–1974 on pages 6–21.

4. For Paul Otlet, see his *International Organization and Dissemination of Knowledge: Selected Essays,* trans. and ed. W. Boyd Rayward (Amsterdam: Elsevier, 1990). For microfiche see pp. 87–95 and for the microphotographic library see pp. 204–13. Also see W. Boyd Rayward, *The Universe of Information: The Work of Paul Otlet for Documentation and International Organization,* FID publ. 520 (Moscow: VINITI, 1976). Robert B. Goldschmidt and Paul Otlet, *La conservation et la diffusion internationale de la pensée: Le livre microphotique,* IIB publ. 144 (Brussels: International Institute for Bibliography, 1925). On p. 6 Otlet and Goldschmidt note that electronic telecommunications had great potential for access to documents: "Que ne réserve la télévision après les découvertes récentes?"

5. Fritz Donker Duyvis' comment is on p. 53 of his "4th Report of the 'Commission internationale de la Classification Décimale,'" *Documentation Universalis* 1/2 (1931):46–54.

6. Fremont Rider, *The Scholar and the Future of the Research Library: A Problem and Its Solution* (New York: Hadham Press, 1944), 99. See also Lodewyk Bendikson, "When Filing Cards Take the Place of Books," *Library Journal* 58, no. 20 (15 Nov. 1933):911–13.

7. See, for example, Robert S. Casey and others, eds., *Punch Cards: Their Application to Science and Industry*, 2d ed. (New York: Reinhold Publishing Co., 1958), 74–81.

8. Microfilm selectors were first described in English in E. Goldberg, "Methods of Photographic Registration," *British Journal of Photography* 79 (2 Sept. 1932):533–34. Michael K. Buckland, "Emanuel Goldberg, Electronic Document Retrieval, and Vannevar Bush's Memex," *Journal of the American Society for Information Science* (Forthcoming, 1992).

9. Robert T. Jordan, *Tomorrow's Library: Direct Access and Delivery* (New York: Bowker, 1970).

10. Michael K. Buckland, *Book Availability and the Library User* (New York: Pergamon, 1975). Paul Kantor, "Availability Analysis," *Journal of the American Society for Information Science* 27 (Sept.–Oct. 1976):311–19.

3

The Automated Library

We use *Automated Library* to denote a library in which the collections of library materials are primarily on paper but in which the library's *procedures* have been computerized. Libraries are very record-intensive: Not only is each title different, but, for many purposes, the records needed for library operations must necessarily be very concerned with *individual copies* of each title. A circulation system must know precisely *which* copy of *which* volume of *which* edition of *which* title was borrowed by precisely *which* borrower and *when* it is due back. Attributing the loan to some other borrower will not do, nor will substituting the return of some other document, even by the same borrower, be acceptable as a discharge of the loan. Acquisition records need to show precisely how many copies of a given work were ordered from which bookseller and which, if any, have so far been received. A library not knowing which titles it already has (and in how many copies) could not function efficiently. Serials records contain minute details of copies of issues, indexes, binding, and invoices in order to assure that each set is complete and properly acquired, bound, and paid for. Library records, then, must be specific to individual copies.

In general it is desirable that library record-keeping be automated for three reasons:

1. Much of the work involves the accurate updating of records in files. The tasks involved are generally tedious, repetitive, mechanical in nature, and lend themselves to computerization, even though the records may be complex and arranged in complicated ways.

2. Automation is likely to improve cost-effective performance by increasing accuracy, by reducing the rate of increase in costs in labor-intensive activities, and by increased effectiveness. It should become

possible to do some tasks more thoroughly than levels of staffing usually permit with manual procedures, such as the regular claiming of unsupplied issues of periodicals, or by doing things that cannot in practice be done in paper files, notably searching for combinations of characteristics.

3. Automation permits decentralized access to records. A librarian in a branch library can verify the status of an order without maintaining duplicate files, traveling to the order department, or asking other staff to interrupt their work in order to find out. A user can check to see whether a book is out on loan without traveling to the library to see if it is on the shelf.

Considerations of service, of cost, and of the humane use of staff all argue for the use of computers to ease the burden and to increase the effectiveness of handling library records.

STANDARDS

Bringing order to chaos and achieving collaboration both depend on shared understanding: on standards. Library service has long depended on shared standards, of which the adoption of standardized cataloging codes and standardized subject classification schemes are two very important examples. These two examples and most library standards may facilitate automation and make computerized procedures more cost-effective, but they have little to do with computers directly.

Two standards have enormous strategic importance for the Automated Library:

1. The MAchine Readable Cataloging (MARC) communications formats for catalog records define how catalog records (and potentially other bibliographic records) can be communicated from one computer system to another. This national (NISO Z39:2) and international standard (ISO 2709) is now more than twenty years old. Although rather complicated and cumbersome, it provides a degree of standardization in record format that is an essential basis for the economical development of the Automated Library.

2. More recent, much less well-known, but of comparable strategic importance is the "Search and Retrieve" standard, sometimes called the "Linked Systems Protocol" (ISO 10162/10163; US NISO Z39:50).[1] In the first twenty years of the Automated Library a searcher would use *one* on-line catalog or *one* on-line bibliography at a time. After finishing with one system, the searcher could then consult another—one at a time and separately. But as the number of different systems increased, each using commands that were more or less different from the others, and requiring telecommunications to more or less remote sites, the advantages and the

inconvenience of using not only one's local system but also other, different, remote systems became increasingly clear.

The sensible alternative, for anyone interested in using computers, was to try to keep the advantages and to delegate the inconvenience. Instead of withdrawing from one's local on-line catalog in order to use another, one would prefer to command the local on-line catalog to extend the search to other on-line catalogs elsewhere on one's behalf and to retrieve and to present the results. In principle, this removes from the user the need to bother with the telecommunications and possibly unfamiliar commands needed for the other on-line catalogs. (See figure 3.1.) In theory any remote on-line catalog can become an extension of the user's local catalog with the differences in commands made largely transparent. Getting one computer to "Search and Retrieve" from another can, in principle, be extended to a variety of bibliographic files (circulation, acquisitions, bibliographies, and so on). This is a new development. By 1991 the national and international standards were being revised to achieve compatibility, software developers had formed a Z39:50 implementors group, and early versions were becoming available.

The MARC standard enables computer-based bibliographic data to be shared and the "Search and Retrieve" standard enables retrieval systems to be shared. The long-term consequences of both are enormous.

a. Without the "Search and Retrieve" protocol a user can connect with various on-line catalogs and must know how to use each

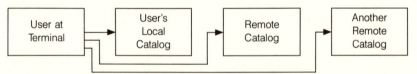

b. With the "Search and Retrieve" (Z39:50) protocol, the user need only know how to use the local catalog and how to instruct it to extend a search to other systems

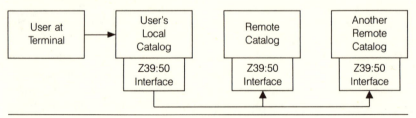

Figure 3.1. "Search and Retrieve" (Z39:50) protocol

TECHNOLOGICAL TRENDS

Those who predict technological trends are unanimous on certain points. If, for lack of any grounds for doing otherwise, we accept their projections and extrapolate them forward for a few years, we reach some simple planning assumptions concerning the new information technology:

1. Improved performance by computers, if continued, will result in computing power becoming extremely inexpensive, with a trend toward a computer on every desk.
2. Telecommunications will become ubiquitous, convenient, and very low cost per character transmitted.
3. Data storage costs will become trivial.

Everything else, including labor costs, we should assume to be unchanged or getting worse. Library service is very labor-intensive. About two-thirds of a library's budget usually goes for labor. Since machines can be made more cost-effective in a way that human beings cannot, it appears inexorable that the cost of labor will tend to increase relative to other costs as shown in figure 3.2.

Because of the steadily shifting relationship between machines and humans, we can expect the amount of machine use to increase steadily relative to the use of labor for any and all activities for which machines can be used. The effect may simply be empowerment—more machine power to increase what a person can do. The effect will also be one of substitution—what can be delegated to machines will increasingly be delegated as that becomes technically and economically feasible.

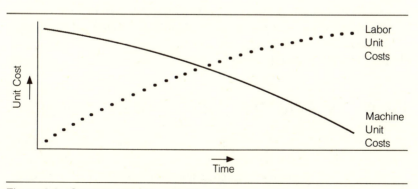

Figure 3.2. Costs trends: labor and machines

"DRIFT-DOWN" PRINCIPLES

The following "drift-down" principles have been proposed by Michael Gorman:

1. Nothing should be done by a professional that can be done by a technician.
2. Nothing should be done by a technician that can be done by a clerk.
3. Nothing should be done by a human being that can be done by a machine.[2]

These principles do not necessarily apply in all circumstances but they do seem reasonable guidelines for improving the cost-effectiveness of library services in North America.

EXPERIENCE WITH LIBRARY AUTOMATION

Paper Libraries of any size now either are or are becoming Automated Libraries. We have some familiarity with what is involved. In brief, the change from the nineteenth-century design of the Paper Library to the Automated Library has been characterized by

standardization of data,
remote access to files,
the linking and combining of files,
access to numerous different files from the same terminal,
increased cooperative use of shared files,
discontinuation of numerous, more-or-less duplicative local files,
greater capability for doing things to and with the (computer-based) files, and
increased vulnerability to technological failure.

PROBLEMS OF THE AUTOMATED LIBRARY

The Automated Library perpetuates some of the problems of the Paper Library noted in the previous chapter. Because the collections of documents are still on paper, a localized medium, the need for local collections, the space needed for paper documents, the inflexibility of paper documents, the separation of documents from the users, the limitations associated with the opening hours for the collections (though no longer for the catalog), and the competition for use of copies of documents all remain as much a problem in the Automated Library as in the Paper Library. The catalog may be used in a number of places. In particular, with remote access to the on-line catalog, the user is no longer separated from the catalog, and the separation of catalog and documents is somewhat diminished since, on-line, a catalog can at long last be used in the book stacks.

The Automated Library represents a significant improvement but for only some of the problems and, aside from the on-line catalog, benefits directly those who are *providing* the service rather than those who are *using* the service.

Notes

1. Michael K. Buckland and Clifford A. Lynch, "The Linked Systems Protocol and the Future of Bibliographic Networks and Systems," *Information Technology and Libraries* 6 (June 1987):83–88; Michael K. Buckland and Clifford A. Lynch, "National and International Implications of the Linked Systems Protocol for Online Bibliographic Systems," *Cataloging & Classification Quarterly* 8 (1988): 15–33.

2. Michael Gorman, "The Organization of Academic Libraries in the Light of Automation," *Advances in Library Automation and Networking* 1 (1987):152.

4

Bibliographic Access Reconsidered

This chapter draws attention to on-line bibliographies and suggests that the combination of on-line bibliographies and on-line library catalogs will lead to a radical change in how the catalog is defined and constructed. Also, instead of thinking of on-line bibliography as the use of individual bibliographies that happen to be on-line, we shall think more in terms of on-line use of a reference collection.[1]

BIBLIOGRAPHY AND BIBLIOGRAPHIC ACCESS

The term *bibliography* is used in several ways to denote the study of books and the making of descriptions of books. Here we are concerned with bibliography as the making of lists of books, articles, and other documents—by subject, by author, and by other attributes—and the making of indexes to those lists.[2]

Bibliographic access is perhaps the best available term for the whole apparatus of access to records of all kinds (textual, numerical, visual, musical, etc.) in all kinds of storage media (books, journals, microform, computer storage, disks, and so on). Examples of the sorts of bibliography under discussion include *Chemical Abstracts, Annual Review of Information Science and Technology, Books in Print, Readers' Guide to Periodical Literature,* and the *Arts and Humanities Citation Index.*

Bibliographic access includes three central concerns:

1. *Identifying documents:* Which documents exist that might be of interest? The essence of bibliography is the identification and enumeration of

documents that would be of interest: Which writings by some specified author? Which articles about some subject? Which books published in some time, place, or language? It is a matter, on the one hand, of creating useful descriptions of documents, and, on the other, of identifying documents that fit any given description.

2. *Locating documents:* Bibliographies describe documents, but they do not usually tell you where a copy can be found, least of all where the nearest copy can be found. It is catalogs that indicate where copies may be found. During the nineteenth century catalogs became more elaborate in their descriptions and came to look like and, indeed, to be bibliographies of local holdings. The differentiating characteristic of a catalog is that it indicates a location. If it did not we should deny that it is a catalog.

3. *Physical access to material:* Identifying and establishing the supposed location of a document is not the same as having a copy of the document in the searcher's hands, close enough to read. As Eric Moon, former president of the American Library Association, remarked, "I never knew a reader who wanted a book 'right now' who left the library wildly enthused by finding a catalog entry for it."[3] Physical access—some combination of the user going to the document or the document being brought to the user—is a matter of logistics and technology that we shall discuss in Chapter 6.

BIBLIOGRAPHIES

The components of the bibliographical universe are numerous as well as varied. Besterman's *World Bibliography of Bibliographies* lists 117,187 bibliographies and is restricted to an incomplete enumeration of separately published bibliographies.

An important feature of bibliography in this sense is that it is primarily concerned with works and editions of works rather than with individual copies of documents. A bibliography on academic freedom might well include a reference to, say, David P. Gardner's *The California Oath Controversy,* but the reference is to the work, and, usually, to a specific edition of a work. Bibliographies are not ordinarily concerned with specific copies of an edition. Information about individual copies is usually included only in exceptional circumstances: one copy is somehow different (a bibliographical variant), or it may be the only extant copy known. For rare materials and early printing it is customary to note where individual copies can be found or which individual copy was inspected by the bibliographer. Nevertheless, as a general rule, bibliography deals with published editions rather than with individual copies of an edition.

Because bibliographies describe works rather than individual copies, they are of general interest to anyone who might benefit from knowing of the works that are listed. For this reason publication of, or at least widespread public access to, bibliographies is highly desirable.

Bibliographies, especially continuing ones, lend themselves well to computer-based production, which reduces the tedium of the mechanical tasks of sorting, cumulating, updating, rearranging, and indexing a large number of individually brief records. It has become difficult to imagine creation of a bibliography without using a computer and the logical next step to make the bibliography available on-line.

It is reasonable to expect the number of bibliographies available in machine-readable form to increase and for them to account for a growing proportion of all use of bibliographies. It is also reasonable to expect that these bibliographies will become available in more different ways: accessible through commercial database services; available as tapes that can be mounted at computer centers; or available on optical digital disks, such as CD-ROMs, attachable to microcomputers.

The next logical development would be to provide links from the references in the bibliographies to the holdings records of libraries. If one were to find an interesting reference to an article while searching *Chemical Abstracts* on-line, for example, it would be an obvious amenity if one could move automatically from the bibliographic reference to a statement of local libraries' holdings of the periodical concerned. This kind of service is beginning to be provided. Even better, one would like to know whether that particular volume is currently available and to be able to send a request for a copy of it.

THE CATALOG RECONSIDERED

Bibliography, as noted earlier, deals with published works in a general fashion and is not ordinarily concerned with individual copies of works. In contrast, library records are, of necessity, very much concerned with individual libraries, individual copies, and, for that matter, with individual library users.[4]

Library catalogs, as we currently know them, are composed of a combination of bibliographic records and of library holdings records, containing both general statements about editions of works and also specific statements about individual copies and their individual locations in particular libraries. One might even argue that, given the limitations of the technology of paper and of cardboard, the only practical way of achieving this linking of bibliographies and library records in the nineteenth century was to create an additional third set of records containing elements derived from each: the modern library catalog.

Library catalogs vary considerably in format according to the technology in use: in book form, on cards, in microform, or on-line. Further, if library catalogs are seen as a bridge between bibliographies and library records, it has to be recognized that this is a bridge between two moving and changing objects as bibliographies and internal library procedures both evolve.

Early library catalogs were inventories of what was on the shelves. The printed catalog of 1620 of the Bodleian Library of Oxford University is regarded as significant because it listed books in author order regardless of where they were shelved. This, then, was the library catalog as an author-ordered finding list of books.

The transformation of library cataloging to its present form came in the nineteenth century when it was argued that simple author access was not enough and that a different, more sophisticated, and more elaborate approach was needed.

The classic definition of the purpose of a library catalog is that of the nineteenth-century librarian Charles A. Cutter, who stated that the "objects" of a catalog are:

1. To enable a person to find a book of which either
    (A) the author
    (B) the title   } is known.
    (C) the subject
2. To show what the library has
    (D) by a given author
    (E) on a given subject
    (F) in a given kind of literature [poetry, drama, fiction].
3. To assist in the choice of a work
    (G) as to its edition (bibliographically)
    (H) as to its character (literary or topical).[5]

In effect, the new library techniques of the mid and late nineteenth century can be viewed as building up on top of simple finding lists a superstructure of bibliographical access: complex subject headings, added entries, cross references, systematic shelf-arrangements, and so on.

The form of display moved from catalogs in book form to catalogs in card form, which are easier to update, but the principal change was the local development of more elaborate access to the contents of the collection. Modern library catalogs are essentially as defined in the nineteenth century.

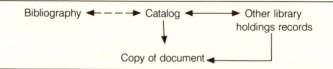
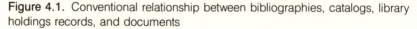

Figure 4.1. Conventional relationship between bibliographies, catalogs, library holdings records, and documents

A catalog includes an essential element that is normally absent from bibliographies, the call number, although this is in practice an incomplete and imperfect reflection of the precise status of the library's holdings. To determine the actual status it may also be necessary to refer to library holdings records: to the circulation file for the best information on what is where, to serials records to know which pieces have arrived, to the "in process" file to know what has arrived but has not yet been cataloged, and to acquisitions files to know what is believed to be on its way. Although the catalog may show that the library has a book, the book may have been lost.

The present set of relationships can be expressed as follows: Records found in bibliographies may help one find corresponding records in catalogs, if present, and vice-versa. The catalog usually indicates the official location of a copy of a document. But one may choose to (or need to) consult other library holdings records (acquisitions, circulation, serials) for more precise information concerning actual copies of documents and their locations. The present relationship between bibliography, library records, and the catalog is shown in figure 4.1.

In terms of Cutter's definition of the purpose of a library catalog, almost all of the data needed are bibliographical and would be common to any other library catalog or bibliography that listed the same edition. The exception is the locational information: the particular call number and details of each copy, as needed. The locational data would not be the same as those found in other libraries' catalogs listing the same work.

The Catalog as a Form of Bibliography

In the broader perspective of bibliographic control, library cataloging can be seen as a special case of bibliography defined by the intersection of two subsets.

1. Library catalogs use one particular level of description: the edition of the monograph and the title of the periodical. More detailed ("analytical") cataloging is possible and can be found, especially in small, specialized libraries, but it is not typical.

2. The set of records in a library catalog is further defined geographically: the records that pertain to the holdings of a collection, of a library, or, for a "union catalog," of two or more libraries.

It is important to stress that the limitation by level of description (monograph edition, journal title), which excludes the more detailed levels of access (journal article, conference paper) commonly needed, is a matter of standard practice, not of principle. Excellent examples can be found of library catalogs that also provide entries for articles in periodicals and individual contributions within books. One example is the *Index-Catalogue of the Library of the Surgeon-General's Office, United States Army*, published in 1880, which evolved into the *Index Medicus* and now *MEDLINE*. Another published example is the *Catalogue of the Library of the Peabody Institute of the City of Baltimore*, 1883–1892, which states in the Preface:

> This catalogue is constructed on the idea that the best possible catalogue is that which best makes known to the average reader the entire contents of a library. It is intended to answer the three important questions: Is a given book in the library? Are the works of a given author there? Which books, articles, and information does a library contain on a given subject? A perfect catalogue would furnish complete answers to all these questions.[6]

However, technical and cost considerations resulted in the general practice of omitting detailed ("analytical") access, especially to articles in periodicals, leaving that important role to publishers of bibliographies and indexes who operate mainly outside of librarianship.

Library catalogs should be seen as a form of bibliography. That they are not normally thought of as bibliography is largely an accident of semantic custom and of a tradition of library organization that associates the catalog with catalogers in technical-services departments and bibliography with reference librarians in public-services departments.

From an operational perspective the library catalog can be seen as a useful amplification of records that are unavoidably needed anyway. The information in a catalog can be useful in a variety of ways to library staff and library users. The difference between modern library catalogs and those before the late nineteenth century is essentially that the modern catalogs have a much larger bibliographical superstructure added to the locational information than had previously been the case.

However, a library catalog has some significant shortcomings as a tool of access. In contrast, published bibliographies are, or can be

more complete (extending beyond a given library's collections),
more selective (focusing on the interests of specific clientele and so, in the terminology of information retrieval, of "higher precision"),

more capable of special arrangements (as opposed to standardized universal schemes of classification and of subject headings),

more flexible (because each new bibliography can be done differently),

more detailed (indicating individual papers within periodicals, articles in newspapers, and papers within conference proceedings),

more descriptive (containing abstracts of the contents),

more easily deployed to cover new topics of interest as needed,

more expertly compiled (because bibliographers are more likely than catalogers to be expert subject specialists),[7]

more coherent (because bibliography starts with a topic around which selected references are assembled; whereas, in cataloging, documents are assigned to subjects),

more cost-effective (because a bibliography's usefulness is not limited to an individual library).

Catalogers have denied these assertions and made counterarguments that, for example, local cataloging (unlike bibliographies published for a general audience) permits access to be adapted to local circumstances and can include items not included in published bibliographies.

In the late nineteenth-century debate between bibliographers and catalogers, bibliographers unsuccessfully argued that the investment made in local library cataloging would be better spent in the improvement of bibliographies that could be published and would be, therefore, of widespread usefulness.

Raynard Swank wrestled with how libraries could combine the advantages of bibliographies with the necessity of local records. A sufficient reason why he was unsuccessful was that, in the last resort, the technology of paper and of cards simply did not lend itself to the physical integration of bibliography and catalog. Subject bibliography (other than cataloging) has developed during the twentieth century largely outside the mainstream of librarianship, with major roles in the creation and provision of access to bibliography played by individual scholars, professional and scholarly societies, government agencies, and private firms (such as Bowker, Lockheed, and Wilson).

Two Perspectives Caricatured

The difference between a bibliographer's perspective and that of a cataloger can be illustrated by considering how each might approach the provision of bibliographical access to, say, a chemistry library. Both fantasies are exaggerated for the sake of emphasis.

A bibliographer responsible for a chemistry library might take the point of view that there is a published bibliography of the literature of chemistry that should be the users' principal tool of access to the entire relevant literature including the subset that happens to be held in a particular library. The strategy might then be to arrange for plentiful use of *Chemical Abstracts,* perhaps by mounting a copy on-line locally, then seeking to link the citations in *Chemical Abstracts* to the library's holdings records. Perhaps the link could be made by using the International Standard Serials Number (ISSN) for each periodical title and the Library of Congress catalog card number (LCCN) or International Standard Book Number (ISBN) for each monograph. In the meanwhile the library's records would also have ISSN, LCCN, ISBN, or similar numbers attached. (This technique is suggested as evidence that linkage is feasible. Other approaches are possible but outside our present scope.) In this scenario, the library user would search *Chemical Abstracts* and be able to ascertain the library's holdings when interested. Possibly, as an option, searches could be automatically limited, at least initially, to entries with links to library holdings records. Alternatively, that subset with library holdings links could be separated as an unusually detailed "catalog" of locally held material. Locally held material not or not yet in *Chemical Abstracts* would pose a problem. Possibly such material could be contributed to *Chemical Abstracts* if it was on chemistry; perhaps other bibliographies would need to be used for other subjects. Some local supplementation of the files would probably be unavoidable. (This linking of a bibliography with library holdings records has been implemented experimentally for the medical and health sciences for the nine campuses of the University of California by adding recent years of the MEDLINE bibliography to the on-line catalog.[8])

A cataloger setting out to provide access to locally held materials might also note that a traditional library catalog provides almost no direct access to the literature of greatest interest: the individual papers on chemistry, usually published as articles in periodicals. From a cataloger's perspective it would seem logical and traditional to expand the catalog by cataloging each of the articles in the periodicals received by the library and only in those specific periodicals. The cataloging would be based on national standards but would be adapted to local needs. A significant concern in each library would be the maintenance of local authority control (i.e., consistency in the use of the author and subject headings as modified to suit local needs). Possibly with modern technology and the traditions of interlibrary cooperation, costs would be reduced by using a consortial approach to catalog construction. A shared database of catalog descriptions of articles, technical reports, and books could be developed for chemistry-library catalogs, an "on-line chemistry-library center," perhaps. Catalog records contributed by one chemistry library would be available as a convenient basis for the derivation of records for the local catalog. This cooperative database, with much broader coverage than any one library, would be available to the librarians but not, in practice, to library users. *Chemical Abstracts* would be of greatly reduced value because it would duplicate catalog records for everything in the library.

This small vignette identifies the extravagance of a catalog-based approach compared with a bibliography-based approach and invites more extensive examination of the potential role of bibliographies in the future of the catalog.

THE CATALOG REDEFINED

Reconstruction

How should the identification and location functions be approached in the future? To the extent that the card catalog was a product of the limitations of what is no longer the preferred technology, the development of even the most sophisticated electronic version of the card catalog could represent misguided creativity, reminiscent of the continued refinement of sailing ships after steam had become the preferred source of power. To get a better perspective on future library service we should stand back from the conventional catalog and try to view it from first principles.

Three elements—bibliography, library records, and documents—provide the needed ingredients. Bibliographies will continue to be published; documents continue to be collected; and libraries have to have their copy-specific inventory and status records. Computer-based procedures enable records to be linked in ways not previously feasible. The following approach is suggested:

1. Since bibliographies constitute the principal means of identification, there should be extensive, convenient access to bibliographies regardless of technology.

2. Because it is necessary not only to identify but also to locate material, it should be made possible when searching bibliographies to ascertain the location, call-number, and availability of copies of documents in local library holdings.

3. It would be convenient to have an option whereby searches in bibliographies could be limited to the holdings of one or more particular libraries.

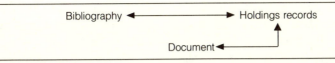

Figure 4.2. Simplified relationship between bibliographies, holdings records, and documents

4. It should also be possible for a library user to forward a copy of a bibliographic record to library staff as a request that a copy of the document represented be sent in the original, in photocopy, or by telefacsimile.

These relationships are represented in figure 4.2.

There are practical problems to be solved in linking bibliographies with holdings records of libraries. However, there appears to be no obvious technical reason why on-line bibliographies should not routinely be linked to holdings records, call-numbers, and circulation status for documents. Once that is appreciated who would want to settle for less?

Another way of describing this change in the relationship between bibliographies, catalogs, and library holdings records can also be shown in terms of the contents of the records involved. Part a of figure 4.3 shows the conventional records structure of figure 4.1. Part b of the figure shows the simplified structure of figure 4.2.

a. Conventional record structure for bibliography, catalog, and library holdings records

| Access points | Bibliographical record | | | Record in a bibliography for an edition |

| Access points | Bibliographical record | Copy/location data | | Catalog record for an edition with copy and location data |

| Access points | Copy/location data | Other data | | Basic record type for library holdings records (acquisitions, in process, circulation) |

b. Simplified record structure for linked bibliography and library holdings records

| Linking number | Access points | Bibliographical record | | Record in a bibliography for an edition, with linking number, e.g., ISBN or ISSN |

| Linking number | Access points | Copy/location data | Other data | Basic record type for library holdings records (acquisitions, in process, circulation), with linking number |

Figure 4.3. Conventional and linked record structures

The use of computer-based techniques to achieve the goal of extensive bibliographical access *combined with* call-number and availability information for documents invites a major reconsideration of the roles and relationships between library collections, bibliographies, and internal library processes:

1. Bibliographies should be viewed not merely as library resources, but rather as a dramatic enrichment of bibliographic access far greater than can be provided by the catalog. Not only does the access provided by bibliographies greatly exceed that of catalogs in fineness of indexing but also in the sheer quantity of records and their variety. Nontrivial intellectual access to the published record *depends* on access to bibliographies. Conventional catalog records, limited as they are to editions of monographs and titles of serials and to locally owned material only, are simply not in the same league in terms of providing bibliographical access.

2. Operating records of libraries (acquisitions, circulation, serials receipts, etc.) should be automated whenever feasible. In the case of acquisitions, circulation, and other useful information, these records should be made accessible to users and to other libraries, to the extent security and privacy considerations permit.

3. The records in bibliographies will need to be linked to the libraries' holdings records. This implies some changes. Neither the traditional marketing through centralized retailers (e.g., DIALOG) nor the newer, isolated, "stand-alone" systems on CD-ROMs deliver what is needed. Either could do so if standardized interfaces to local libraries' records were provided. Another likely option is for libraries to mount on-line bibliographies locally in conjunction with their library-automation systems. A bibliographical search would continue to be a two-stage process, as it is with manual searching: first to identify what exists, then to locate a copy. The difference would be that computer-based procedures should be designed not only to handle each stage but also the transition between them. It would be a natural and logical extension of the "Search and Retrieve" protocol (NISO Z39:50) to have a standard interface whereby a set of bibliographical records retrieved from a bibliography could be searched against a set of library records. This would include three separable tasks: transferring back the retrieved set of references from a bibliography, searching that set against a file of library holdings records, and coping with data deficiencies in either file that would impede matching (e.g., lack of linking numbers).

Given the roles and relationships described in the preceding paragraphs, two views of the future of the library catalog emerge. From one point of view, *the library catalog, as we currently know it, becomes obsolete.* Given an ability to link records in bibliographies to holdings records, there is no longer any role for the catalog to play. This is entirely to be expected if one accepts that it was the limitations of the technology of paper that prevented the effective combining of bibliographies with library records; the solution adopted in the nineteenth century (and still in use) was to create in the catalog what is, in effect, an alternative local bibliographical structure, a duplicative set of bibliographical records that are also present in bibliographies; and the limitations of the technology of paper and of cardboard are ceasing to be relevant as the newer, more flexible technology of computers replaces it. From this view we can expect the massive bibliographical apparatus of the catalog to be abandoned.

Yet, viewed another way, what we can see is a *redefinition* of the catalog as the totality of bibliographic records made available by a library *that can be linked to holdings records*. In this view the "new" catalog blossoms as a means of providing access to the works in a library with a richness of detail to match the nineteenth-century catalogers' most ambitious dreams. This approach is not really inconsistent with traditional catalog practice. A century ago catalogers sought to add entries for parts of books and periodicals. This and the practice of providing annotations stopped only because it was too expensive. In recent years almost all of each library's catalog records have been copied, through cooperative arrangements, from the Library of Congress card service, from large shared databases of catalog records, or elsewhere. Even "original" cataloging is usually derived from (or verified against) extant bibliographic records as far as is practical.

The many different forms of subject indexing found in bibliographies is a complication. Users with specialized interests should benefit more from specialized indexing than from the standardized approach to subject cataloging used in general (and many specialized) libraries. Attempting to harmonize a babel of different kinds of subject headings, indexes, and classification schemes would pose serious difficulties. This variety is already present in existing bibliographies, but without the benefit of links to holdings records. The possibility of providing library users not only with extensive, convenient on-line access to a wide range of bibliographies but also with interconnected access to bibliographies, catalogs, and libraries holdings is an exciting prospect.

Multiple Locations

New developments in telecommunications enable on-line catalogs (and on-line bibliographies) to be consulted from a distance. One consequence is that it becomes possible for several libraries to share the same catalog, should they wish. A union catalog brings together the records of two or more libraries, whether a union catalog for all branches of a single system, a shared on-line catalog for two or more different library systems, or a resource of catalog records (notably OCLC, the On-line Catalog Library Center, in Dublin, Ohio) for catalogers and interlibrary loan staff.

Another consequence is that it becomes possible for the user of one library to use the on-line catalog of another, remote library ("remote access"), though formalities of telecommunications, passwords, and unfamiliar commands may make it more or less inconvenient to do so. Since computers can be programmed to handle tedious routines, it would make much more sense to tell one's local, familiar on-line catalog to extend any given search to remote, unfamiliar catalogs on one's behalf. The new "Search and Retrieve" ("Linked Systems Protocol") standards (NISO Z39.50; ISO 10162/10163) are designed to facilitate just that. By making any remote catalog a temporary extension of the local catalog, a searcher is, in effect, creating not so much a union catalog but temporary ad hoc *unions of* catalogs as and when needed. This will achieve in the Automated Library what was done in the Paper Library when copies of the printed book-form catalogs of remote libraries were exchanged and collected in reference collections.

Multiple Indexes

Research on information-retrieval effectiveness has shown that different retrieval systems (i.e., different kinds of indexing and classification systems) all work imperfectly, generally work comparably imperfectly, and tend to retrieve different items from the same file. One implication of this research finding is clear: Whether or not one wishes to seek to improve the performance of any given indexing or classification system, it is foolish to rely on any one approach. It is wise to use a multiplicity of approaches and to combine the results. But in the Paper Library maintaining even one subject approach is very onerous. (How many libraries can afford to change systematically all existing catalog entries when revised rules and headings are adopted?) Investing in the creation of multiple approaches in catalogs is *very* expensive. Yet any experienced bibliographer, any experienced researcher, knows that for the best results it is prudent to look in a variety of different sources, and the more different they are in their approach, the better. Libraries in the United States have been able to afford subject headings as well as subject classification, but additional approaches, although clearly desirable, would be unthinkable in the Paper Library.

In the shift from the Paper Library to the Automated Library the technological constraints have changed. Indexing that is merely mechanical can now be provided without investing local labor in its creation. Using the words in titles for "title keyword" searching in an on-line catalog is a good example: Only computer programming and computer hardware need be added, not more cataloging staff. Citation indexes constitute another good example of a useful, mechanical, supplementary approach. Indexing that is not simply mechanical can be obtained, for example, by acquiring bibliographies, and can be used to "enrich" the catalog.

FUTURE BIBLIOGRAPHIC STRATEGY

From Local to General

Since it no longer matters much where a catalog or bibliography is located, a change of perspective becomes possible: Instead of concentrating on the local catalog and locally held bibliographies, one can think more sensibly in terms of making use of *all* bibliographies and catalogs, or, at least, of all "networked" bibliographic resources. In practice this means gaining access to all bibliographic files that are available through networks and held by institutions willing to collaborate.

The basic functional requirements for a more general, networked, collaborative, or universal approach to library collections include the following:

1. The overall bibliographic coverage should be as complete as possible in providing access to the whole of human knowledge.
2. Multiple access points should be provided, minimally by subject as well as author.
3. It should be a distributed system in that everyone should be able to have access to it and in that it should be possible for files to be partitioned and copied for efficiency.
4. Bibliographic records should be correct, concise, correctable, and expandable.
5. This bibliographic universe should be built up piecemeal from existing sources.
6. Bibliographic records should state where copies of the documents are located.
7. The bibliographic records should provide a basis for quantitative studies of publication patterns ("bibliometrics").
8. The bibliographic system should help to protect intellectual property.

These are, with only slight revision, the eight functional specifications for a universal approach to bibliographic control enumerated by Henri La Fontaine and Paul Otlet when they set out in 1895 to develop their Universal Bibliographic Repertory, long before computers became available. Their eventual failure, fifty years and many million cards later, was as much a tribute to the limitations of the technology of paper as it was to the world wars and chronic underfunding that also beset them.[9]

Beyond the Individual Bibliography

Automating *a* catalog or placing *a* bibliography on-line each represents a substantial technological development. But to think only of an individual on-line catalog or of an individual on-line bibliography—even being aware that there are several different on-line catalogs and numerous individual bibliographies available on-line—is to think in terms of the card catalogs and published paper bibliographies of the Paper Library. A major constraint of the technology of paper is that files cannot easily be reformatted, linked, interfiled, or otherwise combined in dynamic ways. This constraint is not characteristic of on-line systems. What if, instead of thinking of individual bibliographies, we were to base our thinking on the knowledge that there are large and growing populations of bibliographies and catalogs on-line, increasingly connected by telecommunications networks, and containing records that can, in principle, be linked, combined, and rearranged? What could happen if instead of thinking of "on-line bibliography" as using *a bibliography* on-line, we were to follow the logic of electronic technology one step further and think instead of *a collectivity of bibliographies* on-line, in effect of using a *reference library*—a sizable universe of bibliographies—on-line?

When considering multiple bibliographies (and catalogs) it can be helpful to think of the various differences between systems:

> Different bibliographies represent different, more or less overlapping populations of documents;
> Different bibliographies will have more or less different descriptions, even for the same document;
> The access points ("indexes") that can be searched vary between systems;
> Different systems can have more or fewer references between different related terms ("See," "See also," and other kinds of cross-references); and
> Different retrieval systems support different types of searching even in the same bibliographic files; some allow complex search requests or searches for keywords, others do not.

So, correspondingly, one can immediately identify five different classes of reasons for extending searches to two or more on-line bibliographies and/or on-line catalogs. Depending on the circumstances, one might want to

| Number of | Number of Files | |
Retrieval Systems	One	Multiple
One	Typical search of bibliography or catalog	One search on multiple files, e.g., DIALOG "Onesearch"
Multiple	Linked systems searching (Z39:50); Postprocessing of retrieved records	Multiple systems accessing multiple files

Figure 4.4. Extended retrieval

1. Extend a search to another bibliography or catalog because what was desired was not found in the first source, and a new population of documents may contain the information.

2. Extend a search to another bibliography or catalog for a document that has been found because differing bibliographic descriptions can be used to accumulate additional information. For example, consider a medical book present in a library catalog, in a medical bibliography, and in a citation index. All three will have somewhat differing bibliographic records for the same document: The catalog will have a standard catalog record and a note of the location of each copy; the medical bibliography may contribute a different, detailed subject description and an abstract; and the citation index can contribute a list of works cited in the book and another list of works that cite the book. *Combining* these descriptions could improve bibliographic access substantially.

3. Extend a search to other access points. Citations have to be searched in a citation index. The ability to search on other features, such as searching by words within a title or abstract or searching by the language or date of the document, varies significantly between systems.

4. Try another system that has a better or different network of cross references.

5. Extend a search to another system because it has special searching abilities, such as identifying pairs of words that occur close to each other, or extend the search by downloading results into a personal computer for more detailed analysis ("postprocessing").

Figure 4.4 summarizes the four combinations that emerge as retrieval is extended from one file to multiple files and from one retrieval system to combinations of retrieval systems.

SUMMARY

Bibliographic access comprises three elements: identifying documents, the realm of bibliographies; locating copies of documents, the underlying purpose of catalogs; and obtaining a copy of a document, the role of document delivery and collection development.

In the late nineteenth century catalogs were made available on cards and an elaborate bibliographic superstructure (and identifying role) was added. After the last two decades of automating existing bibliographies and catalogs, it has become possible to rethink what should be done in terms of the capabilities and constraints of computers rather than those of paper (and card).

The prospect of a new-found ability to link bibliographies and library holdings records suggests a reconsideration of the bibliographic (identifying) elements of catalogs and a new perspective on the use of bibliographies as a dramatic enhancement and, in a sense, a partial replacement for conventional catalogs.

The rise of telecommunications and the flexibility of computers mean that it becomes practical to use bibliographies and catalogs that are at a distance as well as those that are local. It also becomes more feasible to use more indexes than previously. The general effect of these changes is to change the perspective from local to general and to extend our view of on-line searching from searching individual bibliographies to extended searches of multiple bibliographies using multiple retrieval systems. The linking of bibliographic systems through a "Search and Retrieve" standard (Z39:50) provides a basis both for adding access to a greater number of different files and for using additional retrieval techniques on any given file.

These possibilities suggest that, in future library services, bibliographic access could be developed to support, from any workstation anywhere, the kind of searching that could be done, tediously and imperfectly, in a well-equipped reference collection of a very large, research-oriented Paper Library. However, "could be" and "will be" are not the same. Here we have concentrated on questions of design and technology. A complicating factor is that technological change also affects the producers of bibliographies, publishers, vendors of on-line services, and others in the library's environment, as well as the relationships among them. It seems likely that conflicting interests between the stakeholders will prove more of a constraint on the development of future library services than narrower questions of design and technology.

Notes

1. This chapter draws on Michael K. Buckland, "Bibliography, Library Records, and the Redefinition of the Library Catalog," *Library Resources and Technical Services* 33 (1988):299–311.

2. For a good introduction to bibliographic access see Patrick G. Wilson, *Two Kinds of Power: An Essay on Bibliographical Control* (Berkeley, Calif.: University of California Press, 1969); Ronald Hagler, *The Bibliographic Record and Information Technology.* 2d ed. (Chicago: American Library Association, 1991).

3. Eric Moon, "The Tree from the Front," *Library Journal* 89, no. 3 (1 Feb. 1964):574.

4. See Raynard C. Swank for the rival merits of bibliographies and catalogs, "Subject Cataloging in the Subject-Departmentalized Library," *Bibliographic Organization,* ed. Jesse H. Shera and Margaret Egan (Chicago: University of Chicago Press, 1951), 187–99, and his "Subject Catalogs, Classifications, or Bibliographies? A Review of Critical Discussions, 1876–1942," *Library Quarterly* 14 (1944): 316–32. Both are reprinted in Raynard C. Swank, *A Unifying Influence: Essays* (Metuchen, N.J.: Scarecrow Press, 1981).

5. Charles A. Cutter, *Rules for a Dictionary Catalog,* 4th ed. (Washington, D.C.: Government Printing Office, 1904), 12.

6. Johns Hopkins University, Peabody Institute, Library, *Catalogue of the Library of the Peabody Institute of the City of Baltimore* (Baltimore: Friedenwald, 1883–1892), iii–iv.

7. An argument could be made that this is increasingly *not* the case. Libraries now do little cataloging because they can derive cataloging copy from the Library of Congress (and other expert sources) from the "cataloging in publication" copy often found on the verso of title pages, from cooperative databases of catalog records, and in other ways. "Derived" catalog records of higher quality, more completeness, and greater standardization provide a better basis for the developments envisaged in this chapter.

8. Clifford A. Lynch and Michael G. Berger, "The UC MELVYL MEDLINE System: A Pilot Project for Access to Journal Literature through an Online Catalog." *Information Technology and Libraries* 5 (1989):371–83.

9. Available in English in Paul Otlet, *International Organization and Dissemination of Knowledge: Selected Essays,* trans. and ed. W. Boyd Rayward (Amsterdam: Elsevier, 1990), 25–26.

5

The Electronic Library

We use *Electronic Library* to describe the situation in which documents are stored in electronic form, rather than on paper or other localized media. Note that paper copies of electronic documents, or of excerpts from them, can generally be produced for the reader's convenience. However, the essence of the Electronic Library is that documents are stored and can be used in electronic (or similarly machine-readable) form. In this discussion the term "digital" means text in which individual letters, numbers, and other characters, each separately coded by a particular set of bits, and the term "digitized" denotes an image represented by lots of bits. One could well have a digitized image of a page of text, but in that case none of the individual characters would be coded as characters. In some cases where the characters are regularly formed, it may be feasible to use pattern recognition techniques to identify the individual characters within the digitized image and, thereby, to derive a digital version of individual characters in the text from a digitized image of the page. A digital record of a text is more economical and, ordinarily, more useful than a digitized image.

The adoption of computers for libraries' technical operations, the transition from the Paper Library to the Automated Library, can be viewed as an evolutionary development. Much of the change represented, at least initially, the mechanization of previously manual procedures of the Paper Library. Until the provision of on-line catalogs, the changes have been mainly for internal efficiency and for the convenience of library employees. In contrast, the rise of the Electronic Library may seem more revolutionary than evolutionary because of the implications for the provision and use of library services. But is it really so radical a change? What are the impacts on the provision of library service? How are we to achieve a graceful and efficient continuity of service as electronic documents come into use?

Much of what is published nowadays has already existed in machine-readable form because authors commonly use word processors and printers often employ computer typesetting. Frederick Kilgour has characterized the evolution of electronic publishing as being in four stages:

1. preparation of text in machine-readable form for the production of paper copies with subsequent discard of the machine-readable version,
2. publication of paper copies and also in machine-readable form,
3. publication in machine-readable form only, and
4. publication of information in machine-readable form in an encyclopedia-like database.[1]

Nevertheless, the "full text" of documents in machine-readable form has been generally absent from library services until recently, in contrast with the progress made in making bibliographies, catalogs, and numerical data available in electronic form.

ELECTRONIC DOCUMENTS

The characteristics of electronic documents differ greatly from those of paper documents, which were discussed in Chapter 2:

1. Electronic documents are not localized. Given telecommunications connections, an electronic document can be used from anywhere, without the user even knowing where it is stored geographically.

2. In practice several people can use the same database or electronic records at the same time.

3. Electronic documents are easily copied.

4. Documents stored electronically are very flexible. They are easy to revise, rearrange, reformat, and combine with other documents. Hence the popularity of word processing among people who have to create and, more especially, revise documents.

5. Collections of documents stored in electronic form are now less bulky than paper versions. The trend is to even greater compactness.

In each of these five important characteristics, electronic documents are quite different from paper documents.[2]

THE INCREASE OF ELECTRONIC DOCUMENTS

There is a steady growth of documents in electronic form, and access will necessarily have to be provided to them.[3] Databases are increasingly available in (and sometimes only in) machine-readable form. Publishers commonly have or could have the text of their books in machine-readable form even if they may not yet choose to publish them in that form.

The most obvious source of electronic documents is new publications issued in electronic form. But what of the older materials on paper that occupy so many miles of library shelves? Libraries have undertaken a major, systematic effort at the retrospective conversion of older catalog records from cards to electronic records. What of the retrospective conversion of the texts of older paper documents themselves? The idea might seem wildly unrealistic, but there are grounds to believe that, over time, significant and increasing amounts of older material will become available as electronic documents. In selected areas, notably literature, texts have been converted for research purposes: All classical Greek texts and increasing quantities of medieval and modern literary texts are already available in electronic form. Devices have been available for some years that can scan printed material, derive digital versions, and "read" the text out loud for the blind and visually impaired. The same approach can be used to convert paper texts into electronic form as an alternative to keying them when an electronic form of the text is needed for word-processing purposes. These electronic copies are usually discarded or, at least, are not made systematically available. They could be.

The latest fax technology, using the CCITT class IV standards, involves the transmission of pages of documents by means of digitized images of the pages. Interlibrary loans sent by CCITT class IV fax could be stored and, probably, whenever feasible, converted to digital form (i.e., coded as individual characters rather than images of text) for ease of use and economy of storage. Technology exists for copying microfilmed materials into electronic, digitized form, and, once digitized, much of this also could be converted to digital text. Therefore, it is technically feasible that very substantial amounts of older as well as future library material will become available in electronic form whether or not librarians engage in retrospective conversion. Storage costs for electronic documents are decreasing steadily, while the building costs for storing paper documents are not.

PAPER IS BEST EXCEPT . . .

A document on paper, such as a letter or a book, is unquestionably extremely convenient to use compared with other media such as microfilm or floppy disks, at least for most purposes. But, even if we were firmly agreed that paper were the best medium for documents, it is increasingly clear that there are significant exceptions to this rule. Electronic documents, with or without the generation of paper copies, become preferable in the following instances:

1. When documents are highly *volatile*. For example, it is unwise to depend on printed paper versions of highly changeable material such as airplane schedules, stock prices, and currency exchange rates.

2. When *manipulation* of the document is desired. No one would want to have to transcribe (and possibly mis-transcribe) printed numerical data for statistical analysis if the data were already available in electronic form. Similarly, when a text is to be modified, a bibliography revised, or the layout rearranged, the availability of an electronic copy in a standard format for word processing can dramatically reduce the work involved compared with having only a typed or handwritten copy.

3. When *scanning* for names or for particular words or phrases in a lengthy document. Trying to find mention of some thing or person in, say, a multivolume printed work or the run of a periodical is very tedious and error-prone. No one now would want to compile a concordance "by hand" anymore: The first step in concordance making now is the creation of an electronic copy of the text.

4. When light use of *remote material* is needed. For a thorough reading of a document that is not available locally, obtaining a paper copy by interlibrary loan would probably be preferred. If, however, use were light—to check here and there in the document or to skim the document superficially to see whether or not a more careful reading would be warranted—rapid access by telecommunications to an electronic copy could be attractive.

5. When rapid *communication* is desired, especially within a dispersed group that is not conveniently available at the same time and place. The use of electronic mail has considerable advantages over ordinary mail and, for some purposes, over the telephone.

Note that these examples do not include the usual notion of solid, systematic, consecutive reading. They could be regarded as exceptional cases around the fringes of "normal" use of documents, but in some circumstances, as when geographically separated quantitative researchers collaborate, these exceptions could add up to substantial amounts of activity and a significant proportion of total use.[4] Electronic documents add new possibilities for the use of texts and, in this regard, constitute an enhancement that is valuable in its own right.

REINVENTING THE LIBRARY

What are we to do with a document in electronic form? There is little choice but to do the same as we do with a paper document or with a microfilm document:

Catalog it and, as with manuscripts, pay careful attention to which version or state of text it is.
Store it in some accessible place.
Give it a call number.
Ensure that pertinent bibliographic and location data are accessible in or through bibliographic databases.

There seems no real alternative. Given that electronic documents exist and are becoming progressively more important, to ignore them would be to provide a progressively less complete library service. A library administration might choose to retain an exclusive concentration on paper, microfilm, and other localized media, but that would mean that access to electronic documents would have to be found through other channels, such as the computer center. The result would be a split in the provision of library service: the "library" providing access to only some kinds of documents and another organization providing the balance of the library service—access to electronic documents.

The significant difference with an electronic document as compared to a paper document is that if you have the call number it should be possible, from any workstation, to gain access to it remotely, view it, download it, and "use" it. Think how much simpler and quicker it would be if librarians and, even better, library users could obtain their own interlibrary "loans" (now, technically, copies) on a self-service basis, requiring the tolerance but not the time or energy of the staff of the library from which it is obtained. This change would be rather like the change from having closed library stacks, in which library employees had to fetch each book for users, to open stacks in which library users could obtain and examine books by themselves. Similarly, in the Electronic Library, library staff would be mainly concerned with creating and sustaining the system so that users could serve themselves.

Self-service, however, is a mixed blessing. It assumes standardized, intelligible procedures, presupposes some expertise on the user's part, and may make it less easy for the service providers to know what is going well and what is not going well. Yet it may be the only affordable way to support large-scale library use.

PRIOR EXPERIENCE

Fortunately, we already have some familiarity with what to expect in the Electronic Library from our experience with the transition from the Paper Library to the Automated Library and from our experience with on-line bibliographies. The change from the Automated Library to the Electronic Library is an extension of the same changes that have characterized the shift from the Paper Library to the Automated Library (as noted in Chapter 3):

standardization of data,
remote access to files,
the linking and combining of files,
access to numerous different files from the same terminal,
increased cooperative use of shared files,
discontinuation of numerous, more-or-less duplicative local files,
greater capability for doing things to and with the (computer-based)
    files, and
increased vulnerability to technological failure.

Hardly recognized is the fact that many librarians and library users, particularly in academic and special libraries, already do have extensive experience with the Electronic Library through their use of on-line bibliographies. This is because bibliographies tend to occupy an ambivalent position: They are acquired and used primarily to provide access to other documents, but a bibliography is itself a kind of document. Bibliographies added to library collections are "library materials." For more than twenty years there has been a steady shift toward searching bibliographies on-line as well as or instead of on paper. Although not usually viewed as such, this is an early, incomplete manifestation of the Electronic Library with which there is already substantial experience and familiarity. Hence we should expect the future expansion of the Electronic Library to be an expansion of what is already familiar.

BIBLIOGRAPHIC ACCESS IN THE ELECTRONIC LIBRARY

The advent of text in electronic form, the step from the Automated Library to the Electronic Library, has two profound consequences for bibliographic access and catalog design. First, card catalogs are, necessarily, physically separate from the physical (paper) documents that they describe. Given the technology of paper and of cardboard, it could not be otherwise. Further, *use* of the documents involves physical handling, often borrowing. However, to the extent that both catalog and text are in machine-readable form, both would be remotely accessed from the same workstation and the former physical separation between catalog and text becomes unnecessary—or, at least, transparent and irrelevant to the library user, who should be able to move effortlessly between catalog and text. The catalog might be searched and one or more catalog records retrieved. Then the user might want to examine the contents of a book. A book on paper is more than a mere string of characters since there is an extensive internal structure of references: from the table of contents to chapters and sometimes sections within chapters, from the index entries to numerous points in the text, and, often, internally from one part of the text to another. (Texts in electronic form with this connective apparatus are known as "hypertext."[5] Here, again, the basic ideas were anticipated early in the century by Paul Otlet and his "monographic principle," but the constraints of the technology of cardboard, loose-leaf binders, and cutting and pasting simply do not lend themselves to effective hypertext.[6])

In an on-line world the user could move to the table of contents by depressing a key, then move on to examine a chapter. Next the user might want to look on-line for specific terms or names in the index, then move to specific patches of text, again on-line. Since the text is on-line, the user could expect a concordance providing access to all of the text. The user might abandon that text, follow up a reference (from inside the text or from a citation index) to another text, go back to the catalog records to look for another book, or scan the subject headings with a view to reformulating the search. There would be a continual changing, "zooming in" and out between a broad view and a focus on details. It is not that the familiar data elements of the catalog record will have disappeared or that the identifying and locating functions are any less important, but rather that the catalog will effectively have disappeared as a recognizably separate, physical entity. Instead, the catalog data would be part of a much broader set of data elements and the catalog function would have become one feature in a suite of related functions in on-line library use.

The second consequence for bibliographic access and catalog design in an Electronic Library is that the traditional justification for having a catalog begins to disappear. Historically a library catalog was a guide to local *holdings*. Yet for a library user what matters is convenient *access* to texts. With documents on paper, what is locally owned *is* (approximately and imperfectly) what is conveniently accessible. In practice, studies have shown that, at least in university libraries, users typically cannot find 40 percent of locally owned material on the shelves when they seek it. However, with convenient telecommunications, the physical location of an electronic text is substantially irrelevant. Databases (which are copied, not borrowed) at a distance could be more reliably accessible than paper documents owned by a local library. What is needed, then, is a bibliography, or union catalog, of what is conveniently accessible rather than the much narrower concept of a catalog of what happens to be locally stored.

Three elements—documents, bibliography, and holdings records—remain the needed elements: Documents becoming available in electronic form will need to be stored somewhere; bibliographies will continue to be published; libraries, as documents stores, have to have their copy-specific inventory and status records. In the previous chapter we concluded that since bibliographies constitute the principal means of identification, there should be extensive, convenient access to bibliographies regardless of technology; and, because it is necessary not only to identify but also to locate material, it should be made possible, when searching bibliographies, to ascertain the call-number and availability of documents.

Because of the nature of paper, in the Paper Library and in the Automated Library *conveniently accessible* meant, for practical, physical reasons, "locally held." Given some major assumptions about telecommunications and adherence to standards, the close coupling of "conveniently accessible" and "locally held" begins to dissolve with the Electronic Library. Because electronic documents are remotely accessible, it does not matter much to the library user where the documents are located—any more than it matters much to the user of an Automated Library where the disk drives of the on-line catalog are located. There are economic, engineering, and security considerations concerning the storage of electronic records, but these are technical matters for those who provide the service and are of limited concern to the library user. In the Electronic Library "conveniently accessible" ceases to mean locally held. It becomes as foolish to want to limit library users to locally held documents in the Electronic Library as it would be to want to limit cataloging in the Paper Library to documents published in even years.

In order to achieve the central mission of libraries—providing access to documents—references in bibliographies should link directly to and enable immediate reference to available electronic documents. The technical and "architectural" aspects of achieving such linking are outside the scope of this book. However, the general pattern can be seen as an extension of the restructuring discussed in relation to catalogs in Chapter 4. The diagram showing a simplified record structure for the Automated Library in figure 4.3 is repeated in the first part of figure 5.1 and is extended to include linking to an electronic document in the second part of figure 5.1.

There appears to be no obvious technical reason why access to on-line bibliographies and union catalogs should not extend to include the call numbers of electronic documents wherever located—just as we would want the call numbers of local holdings of paper documents in the Automated Library. Who would want to settle for less?

To the extent that texts become available in electronic form, the whole view of library collections changes. The location and ownership of copies of texts becomes a technical detail for librarians but one that is irrelevant to the reader. What counts is what is conveniently accessible. Given modern telecommunications, any attempt to restrict users'

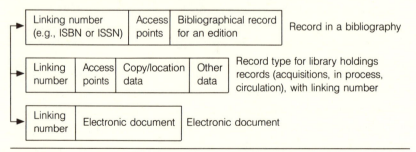

a. Automated Library simplified record structure of linked bibliography and library holdings records

| Linking number (e.g., ISBN or ISSN) | Access points | Bibliographical record for an edition | Record in a bibliography |

| Linking number | Access points | Copy/location data | Other data | Record for library holdings records (acquisitions, in process, circulation), with linking number |

b. Electronic Library simplified record structure of linked bibliography, library holdings records, and documents

| Linking number (e.g., ISBN or ISSN) | Access points | Bibliographical record for an edition | Record in a bibliography |

| Linking number | Access points | Copy/location data | Other data | Record type for library holdings records (acquisitions, in process, circulation), with linking number |

| Linking number | Electronic document | Electronic document |

Figure 5.1. Automated and Electronic Library record structures

attention to locally stored electronic documents would be a travesty of long-established traditions of library service.

THE ARCHITECTURE OF THE ELECTRONIC LIBRARY

What would it take to build an Electronic Library and, indeed, to make Electronic Library service common practice? To develop a library with electronic documents we do not appear to need to draw on anything in librarianship that is different from existing principles. Rather, as with paper and with microform, we have to interpret the same familiar principles in ways appropriate to the technical characteristics of the medium. With electronic documents, even more than with microforms, adherence to standards is important for progress. Electronic documents should themselves be in standard formats. Standards are needed for cataloging electronic documents. Communications formats are needed for conveying electronic documents. Substantial and compatible telecommunications protocols are of great importance. Much work needs to be done in developing and adopting compatible national and international standards for characters, images, documents, telecommunications, and so on. Also, of course, the concept of an Electronic Library assumes a substantial and expensive infrastructure of computing capacity, data storage, and telecommunications, which in turn requires expertise for successful use. These investments are being made anyway in some of the contexts in which library services are being provided.

COEXISTENCE OF PAPER AND ELECTRONIC DOCUMENTS

Although the growth in electronic documents can be expected to be dramatic, the proportion of documents that are available in electronic form (relative to paper documents) will vary greatly from one situation to another. Further, as already noted, for some purposes paper documents are preferable. Not all documents will be available in electronic form. Paper documents are unlikely to disappear, and it is undesirable that they should. So discussion of the Paper Library *versus* the Electronic Library is likely to be of limited benefit. Just a few basic issues are important for planning:

1. Electronic documents are becoming increasingly important and arrangements to provide access to them—the Electronic Library—*must* be developed and is best viewed as additive. The world is changing, and this

additional form of library service appears to be not only desirable for library users but also inevitable.

2. Library services from now on will have to provide access to paper documents *and* to electronic documents according to their users' needs. In other words, library planning should be based on the assumption that all libraries will evolve into some *combination* of an Automated Library and an Electronic Library. The balance between paper documents and electronic documents can be expected to vary widely between libraries and over time. What the balance is at any given place and time matters far less than ensuring that libraries are equipped to provide access to both kinds of documents.

3. The difference between the Electronic Library and the Automated Library is in the technology of the documents, not in the bibliographic access. Bibliographic records need to include information indicating the physical properties of each document (e.g., paper, microform, electronic, optical), but a unified bibliographic approach for all documents is most likely to be helpful. The bibliographic apparatus and internal procedures of the Automated Library would not need to change much for the shift from Automated Library to the Electronic Library. See figure 5.2.

4. The view of the Electronic Library as an *addition* to the Automated Library needs to be modified in two ways. First, purely additive funding should not be assumed. Even though a plausible argument could be made that, in any given case, funding is insufficient to support the Automated Library (as, before it, the Paper Library), nevertheless it is to be expected that service priorities will increasingly lead to a reallocation of total library resources from the Automated Library to the combination of Automated and Electronic Library. In this sense the Electronic Library may well be additive since it is a new form of service, but in its claim to resources it may be subtractive from the Automated Library. It should be a matter of very careful deliberation and consultation to determine when and to what extent, in any given situation, library service should change from being only an Automated Library to being a combination of Automated and Electronic Library service.

Second, in practice there will be some acceptable scope for the substitution of electronic for paper documents, of the Electronic Library

```
┌─────────────────┐
│ The "Catalog":  │─────────────────────── Paper Documents
│ Bibliographic and│────────── Microform and "A/V" Documents
│ Holdings Records │──────────────── Electronic Documents
└─────────────────┘
```

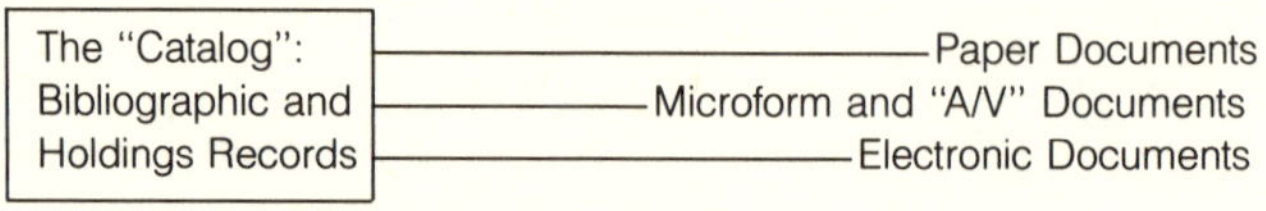

Figure 5.2. Common bibliographic approach

for Automated Library. At some point of adequacy and reliability in on-line catalog service, it becomes reasonable to abandon the card catalog with its high maintenance costs. At some point, in at least some cases, subscriptions to printed bibliographies cease to be justified when on-line versions can be searched conveniently. In the same way, it is reasonable to expect that in some circumstances where there is a choice, access to electronic documents will be preferred to use of paper documents even when the paper version is conveniently available.

The key to consideration of the Electronic Library is recognition that providing access to electronic documents will be needed. How the balance between paper and electronic documents will evolve is an interesting but less urgent issue.

Notes

1. Frederick G. Kilgour, *Beyond Bibliography* (London: British Library, 1985).

2. For a fuller discussion of the implications of texts becoming available in electronic form see Michael K. Buckland, "Library Materials: Paper, Microform, Database," *College and Research Libraries* 49 (1988):117-22.

3. For academic libraries, the following provide convenient introductory reviews of material available in electronic form: Margaret Johnson and others, *Computer Files and the Research Library* (Mountain View, Calif.: Research Libraries Group, 1990); Constance C. Gould, *Information Needs in the Humanities: An Assessment* (Stanford, Calif.: Research Libraries Group, 1988); Constance C. Gould and Mark Handler, *Information Needs in the Social Sciences* (Mountain View, Calif.: Research Libraries Group, 1989); Constance C. Gould, *Information Needs in the Sciences: An Assessment* (Mountain View, Calif.: Research Libraries Group, 1991).

4. For an introductory discussion of the characteristics and acceptability of different media see Brian Shackel, "Information Exchange within the Research Community," in *Information Technology and the Research Process: Proceedings of a conference, Cranfield, 1989,* ed. Mary Feeney and Karen Merry (London: British Library Research, 1990), 147-62.

5. In the terminology of hypertext, cross references (*links*) are made between passages of text (*nodes*) which can, in principle, be text, graphics, animation, or digitized sound. Two or more documents with links between them constitute a *hyperdocument*. A *hypergraph* is a map of *links*. For an introduction to hypertext and its complexity see N. M. Delisle and M. D. Schwartz, "Contexts—A Partitioning Concept for Hypertext," *ACM Transactions on Office Information Systems* 5 (1987): 168-86.

6. Paul Otlet, *International Organisation and Dissemination of Knowledge: Selected Essays* (FID 684). (Amsterdam: Elsevier, 1990).

6

Collections Reconsidered

THE PROBLEM

The shift from the Paper Library to the Automated Library, as discussed in Chapter 4, has raised interesting basic questions about the design and role of the library catalog. It is not simply that the appearance and form of presentation of records in printed book-form catalogs and on three-by-five-inch cards need to be changed for on-line display. A much more fundamental reconstruction of our view of the catalog and, especially, of the relationship between bibliographies and catalogs will eventually follow from the radical change in the underlying technology. The widespread practice during the 1970s and 1980s of using sophisticated computer systems and telecommunications networks to generate three-by-five-inch cards to be filed by hand in card catalogs made sense only as a transitional stage. Designs and approaches that are optimal with one technology are unlikely to remain optimal with a quite different technology.

Do similarly interesting basic questions arise concerning library collections when the documents are electronic rather than on paper? We have already stressed the importance of local collections for the Paper Library. Further, developing a library collection is an attractive activity. How else do you get to spend lots of money buying *and keeping* interesting things . . . using other people's money?

Collection development is also unusually interesting because so much money is involved. It is not only a matter of the funds used to pay for materials, but also the substantial proportion of a library's labor that is devoted to selecting, purchasing, cataloging, and processing the materials, plus associated administrative overhead and space needs for these people and for housing the collection. In the nine campuses of the University of California, for example, two-thirds of the libraries' operating budget and two-thirds of the libraries' space needs can be attributed to the assembling of collections and preparing them for use.[1] Libraries are chronically short of operating budget and of space, so any activity that accounts for two-thirds of both operating budget and space usage ought to be of great interest. When trying to solve a murder mystery, the traditional advice was "Cherchez la femme," look for romantic interest. When studying organizations it is useful to look at where the money flows.

Our perspective on library service is based on experience with libraries in the form of large collections of books. Perhaps we should be better off if we retreat a bit toward first principles. A good starting point is to ask why libraries develop collections. What role, or roles, do collections play?

THE ROLES OF COLLECTIONS

Why do libraries spend so much of their operating budget and space assembling collections? Collecting material does not *create* material. It only affects where copies are located.[2] Library collection development is a matter of "file organization," concerned with where *copies* of documents are to be located and for how long. Collecting cannot be justified for its own sake but only as a means for the role and mission of the library. The role of library service is to facilitate access to documents and, by extension, to provide service based on the availability of documents. The mission of a library service is to support the mission of the institution or population served. These are, however, general statements that need more detailed interpretation in each case. To justify the investment we ought to have a coherent, explicit, and convincing explanation of why we devote so much effort, money, and space to the assembling and refining of collections of documents and of how the "value-added" benefit of collecting compares with the contributions of other claims on library resources, such as bibliographies and assistance to readers. These basic questions have been rather neglected and, perhaps, taken for granted.

A start can be made by isolating the specific purposes that collections, hence collecting, support:

1. *Preservation role:* Any document that is not collected and preserved is likely to be lost, unavailable to readers both now and in the future. It is difficult to predict what might be of interest to someone in the future. When in doubt it is prudent to preserve nonrenewable resources.

2. *Dispensing role:* The principal reason for most investment in collection development is not preservation but the need to provide convenient

access to materials that people want to see *where* they want to see them. If someone asks to see a book, it is not entirely satisfactory to answer that a copy exists and is being carefully preserved in some foreign national library. The need is for a copy here and now.

The difference between the dispensing role and the preserving role can be imagined by considering the difference between the size of library collections as they are now (or, better, as large as people would like them to be) and the size of libraries as they would be if, nation-wide, only two or three designated copies of each edition were retained for preservation purposes and all other copies were vaporized. Imagine how dramatically the space problems of libraries could be solved—and how detrimental it would be for library service—if only two or three preservation copies were retained. The difference is an indication of the importance and high cost of the dispensing role of library materials on paper.

3. *Bibliographic role:* The use of materials depends on identifying and locating what exists. Bibliographies and the bibliographic superstructure that is built up in our catalogs are created for this bibliographic role. Remember, however, that the bibliographic records that we create, arrange, and search in so many ways are surrogates for the (more unwieldy) original documents. Yet bibliographic records are only small, incomplete representations of the real thing. There is no reason why the original documents should not also represent themselves, sitting on the shelves for all to see the choice that exists. Browsing shelves of documents arranged by subject (or any other) order may not be an entirely satisfactory guide to what exists, but it is one way and, unlike the examination of catalog records, has an enormous advantage: the document itself is at hand.

4. *Symbolic role:* The three roles already mentioned—preservation, dispensing, and bibliographic—do not seem sufficient, even taken together, to explain collection development behavior adequately. Collections also have a symbolic role. Large collections, particularly of special materials, bring status and prestige whether the materials are used or not. The symbolic value of collections and of buildings to house them is, perhaps, more marked in the case of museums but should not be ignored in the case of libraries.

If these are the four purposes of collections of library materials, we need to inquire how the change from paper to electronic media may change how we seek to effect these roles.

TWO CLASSES OF MATERIAL

What would an extraterrestrial have to say about the way library services are provided on Earth? To have reached Earth and to be able to send messages back, the extraterrestrial must be familiar with sophisticated technology and telecommunications but might be unfamiliar with and very intrigued by *paper* as a form of information technology.

Paper is energy-efficient and is fairly robust, but it does have two attributes that limit and dominate the way it is used. First, paper is generally a solo technology: Like a telescope, it is usually best used by only one person at a time. It is frustrating when two or more people try to use the same reference book simultaneously. Second, paper is a localized medium: Paper can be read only if the reader and the paper are in the same place at the same time. True, one can travel to a library at any distance or interlibrary loan can bring a copy of a document. Either action involves inconvenience and delay in order to achieve a situation in which the reader and the paper are in the same place.

Electronic documents, in sharp contrast, can be used by many people at the same time. Who knows or would care how many other people are using an on-line library catalog at the same time? Further, unlike documents on paper, users don't even have to be where a database is. Users do have to have telecommunications connections to databases, but they don't even need to know the physical location of the databases they are using.

This discussion is in terms of paper documents and of electronic documents. Other media such as microforms and clay tablets can be seen as inconvenient variations on paper. In the following discussion we will distinguish between materials that are localized (notably paper) and materials that are not localized (notably electronic documents).

ELECTRONIC AND PAPER COLLECTIONS COMPARED

What does the distinction between localized media (e.g., paper) and nonlocalized media (i.e., electronic) signify for the development of library collections when each role is considered?

1. *Preservation role:* For the preservation of nonrenewable resources, it remains prudent to retain two or more copies as archival copies and to store them carefully at different locations under suitable conditions. The specific techniques for preservation vary with the differing physical media (paper, magnetic tape, microfilm, etc.), but a broadly comparable pattern emerges for the preservation of paper and of electronic documents.

2. *Dispensing role:* The substantial difference in transportability indicates a major change in the dispensing role: a much reduced premium on

local storage compared with storage at a distance. In contrast to the localized media of paper and microform, local storage is no longer a necessary condition for convenient access with electronic collections. As a preview of this situation we can consider on-line catalogs. Filing catalog cards locally is no longer necessary for the catalog to be consulted locally. The reader need not know or care where the disk drives are physically located so long as records appear on the screen. (Local storage may sometimes be desirable on the grounds of economy or reliability, but that is a technical matter, varying as telecommunications, storage, and other costs change, and is a concern for the service provider rather than the service user.) There is, therefore, a fundamental change. To the extent to which materials capable of remote access are used, the historic necessity for local collections ceases to apply. Material will not need to be stored locally, will not be out on loan (because it is copied rather than lent), and will be available wherever the user's workstation is located. Local storage becomes optional rather than necessary. Decisions about what to store locally will depend on several changing, technical and economic factors.

Since local collections can account for two-thirds of operating and space costs, there would appear, in theory, to be substantial potential scope for investment in remote access as an alternative.

3. *Bibliographic role:* It is not yet clear how access to machine-readable text will be provided. However, there is no obvious reason why bibliographic records would not also be stored and linked with the text. If this is the case, then the combination of on-line bibliographic data and on-line electronic documents would appear to have all of the advantages of on-line bibliographies and catalogs combined and the advantages of having immediate access to all of the texts for searching, browsing, serendipity, scanning, and reading. This best of two worlds simply cannot be achieved with localized media on paper and microform.

4. *Symbolic role:* The symbolic and status-bringing role of large and impressive local collections of paper documents cannot be denied. Status and useful function tend to coincide. The prestige of having extensive access to electronic documents is less clear, especially as access to electronic documents will probably be a lot more easily and more equitably achievable than has been the case with paper documents, which always have been very unevenly distributed among groups and geographically. Perhaps the wisest course is to emphasize what is functional and hope that prestige will be achieved as a by-product or in other ways. The alternative approach—major investment is what is prestigious but no longer most functional—becomes questionable.

Of these four roles, it is the dispensing role that stands out as being different when electronic documents are compared with paper documents. The difference is two-fold: It is the dispensing role that accounts for the great preponderance of operating costs and space needs in the Paper Library and in the Automated Library, and it is in the dispensing role that electronic documents promise to be particularly advantageous because local storage, which so dominates the operating and space expenses with paper documents, ceases to be necessary.

So, in principle, it appears that it is the dispensing role in which there is the most to be gained *and* it is also the dispensing role in which change appears most feasible. How and how far such a change would be acceptable for the purposes of library users deserves very careful attention because the stakes are so high.

It becomes important to remember that library users fall into two quite different cases with respect to the dispensing role. The obvious case is when the choice is between use of local collections on paper or access to electronic documents. In practice, this is the limited case of the privileged few. For most people, for most documents, for most of the world, the effective choice is likely to be between remote access to collections of electronic documents or the costs and delays of obtaining paper documents on interlibrary loan because so much material is *not* in conveniently local collections. This is the case even with those few countries that currently have the best library collections. Taking a global view it seems difficult to imagine that the vast preponderance of cities that do not now have splendid public library collections and the vast majority of universities that do not now have excellent collections have much prospect of ever being able to achieve excellence by assembling sufficient local collections of paper documents. For rural areas, smaller institutions, and poorer countries the prospect is hopeless.

It would seem very foolish to expect any scenario involving an "either/or" dichotomy—*only* paper collections or *only* a paperless library. Some balance will be needed between selected materials on paper, presumably the more heavily used and less volatile material, and selective recourse to electronic documents for as much of the rest as available. On such a view one might expect core collections of materials in relatively high use to be collected and held locally ("dispensed") on paper, even if they are also available as electronic documents. Core collections, however, are not where the heavy costs arise. The demand for library materials is very unevenly distributed over collections and so most of the cost of acquisition, processing, and especially storage is attributable to the larger quantities of relatively little-used material.[3]

FROM LOCAL TO NATIONAL COLLECTIONS

Just as the change from the Paper Library to the Automated Library, in conjunction with the rise of on-line bibliographies, changes our perspective on the catalog, so also the rise of the Electronic Library changes our perspective on collecting and local collections. Instead of our thinking being dominated by local collections, as is unavoidable with the Paper Library and the Automated Library, the effect of having electronic documents is to make local storage optional rather than necessary. This means that we can realistically begin to think nationally or, in more technical terms, network-wide—as broadly as there is networked access. Since electronic documents do not need to be locally held and since the needs of users in different locations vary, the most plausible approach is that of viewing the totality of electronic documents as being, in effect, one giant distributed collection, analogous to the huge collectivity of bibliographies and holdings records discussed in Chapter 4.

There is much that has to be studied in these issues: Relatively little attention seems to have been given to comparing the costs of *maintaining* paper collections compared with the costs of maintaining electronic collections. If hardware costs and computing costs continue to come down, then presumably the costs of storing electronic documents must also be trending downward relative to the costs of storing paper documents. Similarly studies will need to be made of the costs and difficulties of accessing remote electronic documents compared with accessing both locally held and remote paper documents. Here again the same assumptions about cost trends would suggest a long-term cost trend favorable to electronic documents. For both types of documents the underlying problem is an "owning versus borrowing" trade-off, but the costs, costs trends, and acceptability appear to be different and to be changing.

Here again the issues are broader than technology, costs, and the preferences of library users. Publishers, booksellers, authors, and, probably, intellectual property rights are also moving into a changed situation as electronic documents permit, in principle, a significant change in library collecting practices and in the use of library materials. A changed "industry" and new policies are to be expected.

Notes

1. The estimate on operating budget is derived from campus reports of actual expenditures from state funds for "library materials" and for "acquisitions and processing." The estimate for space is based on university-wide projections of

space needs rather than actual space use. Both are probably underestimates. The assistance of Dennis E. Smith and Sue Plezia is gratefully acknowledged.

2. This section is based on a more detailed discussion: Michael K. Buckland, "The Roles of Collections and the Scope of Collection Development," *Journal of Documentation* 45, no. 3 (Sept. 1989):213–26.

3. Michael K. Buckland, *Book Availability and the Library User* (New York: Pergamon, 1975).

7

Serving the User

THE LIBRARY USER'S WORK ENVIRONMENT

The people whom libraries are to serve are making increasing use of the new information technology of computers and electronic storage, in addition to the old information technology of pen, paper, and photocopier. The new tools provide powerful options for working with data, text, sound, and images. As examples, consider the reduction in labor now required for sending a message or text electronically to distant collaborators, for the compilation of concordances, for complex simulations and calculations, for image enhancement, and for the analysis of large sets of numeric data. There is, predictably, an increasing departure in information handling from the simple pattern of read, think, then write. Computers are used for so much more than the traditional notion of "computing."

Since library services are provided for people to use, two relationships become important: How will changes in the provision of library services affect library users and what they do, and how should changes in the tasks and work habits of library users affect the provision of library services?

The change from the Paper Library to the Automated Library has been primarily a matter of computerizing the library's internal procedures. There has been little impact on library users and little reason for there to be much, that is, until the on-line catalog began to replace the card catalog. Before that time, users may have noticed improved circulation procedures and, perhaps, better-produced lists of various kinds, but the impact of the move to the Automated Library was mainly internal to the library and independent of changes among library users' working habits.

The on-line catalog has two kinds of impact. For all those who visit the library it is a different sort of catalog, with a keyboard, screen, and a new way of searching to be learned in place of using passive trays of cards.

A different impact has been on the growing proportion of library users whose work habits and working environment have changed to include routine use of computers. For these people the option of remote access to the library's catalog has constituted an important new extension of library service. Not since library catalogs were printed and distributed in book form in the nineteenth century has this kind of catalog access been possible. The fact is that this enhancement of service through the automation of the catalog is of benefit only to those who have the technology to use it.

This second, selective impact—an enhancement of service primarily for those whose work habits and equipment enable them to benefit—is a major characteristic of the shift from the Automated Library to the Electronic Library. The ability of the library to provide access from *within* the library to materials stored electronically and to generate copies on paper is clearly a useful extension of service. It can be symbolized by the provision of printouts of the results of bibliographic searches performed by librarians for library users. However, the ability of the library to arrange for access from *outside* the library to materials stored electronically, such that users with suitable equipment and skills can use these resources by themselves, constitutes a much more substantial extension of library service.

Extensive use of the Electronic Library depends on a change in the work habits and working environment of library users. In many work environments, especially in universities and corporations, and among professionals, administrative employees, and writers generally, it is common to find widespread and increasing use of computers and tele-communications. People who have moved to a personal computing environment for their work *need* the provision of an Electronic Library because the effective conduct of their work is based on access to electronic records.

For these reasons the shift from the Automated Library to the Electronic Library should be associated with and paced by the parallel shift in the "task environment" of the people that the library is to serve. Once library users work electronically they are held back by the lack of remote access to an on-line catalog and by the lack of access to materials in electronic form. The Electronic Library will be useful, but the benefits are not fully achieved until library users work electronically. The old information technology of pen, paper, and, latterly, photocopier did not encourage much departure from library use as "read, think, write." In contrast, the new information technology is transforming the use of library materials, with computer-based techniques for identifying, locating, accessing, transferring, analyzing, manipulating, comparing, and revising texts, images, sounds, and data.

This close coupling of library development with changes in users' work styles requires a new perspective among those responsible for library services. It is sad to have observed that "dial-in" access to on-line catalogs has often been slow in coming, limited in extent, or losing in transmission the internal structure (fields) of the catalog record.

Technical Infrastructure

It now seems foolish *not* to assume for library planning purposes that a significant and increasing proportion of those to be served use a computer and that telecommunications are in place to support extensive connectivity between computers, the library, and databases. It is not difficult to outline what needs to be done: The starting point would be the principle that the kinds of services provided in the Paper Library should be made available for use by those who now use the new information technology. Hence from a computer anywhere a library user should be able

1. To search the library catalog, including all cataloged holdings, without need to refer to additional catalogs on card or on microfiche. The library "catalog" is best seen as a series of concentric circles that include the holdings of the local library, of nearby, and of distant libraries. Within each catalog category, the searcher should have the option of expanding a search to associated files: circulation records, incompletely cataloged materials, and files of materials that are on order.
2. To search in bibliographies and to be able to locate the items listed, whether on paper, on microform, or on-line.
3. To search in directories and reference works.
4. To search for numeric data in social, technical, economic, and scientific databases—and to retrieve conveniently whichever data sets are needed.
5. To search for images and moving images—pictures currently on slides, movies, photos, videotapes—and to retrieve copies for use.

6. To search for texts, whether texts that were already known or those discovered in a catalog or bibliography.

These resources (catalogs, bibliographies, directories, numerical data, images, and texts) should be available for library users at their place of work using the tools with which they normally work, which implies copying in electronic form into personal storage, printing, or ordering a copy of printed material. The resources should suit the user's convenience by being available when needed, requiring minimal effort or formality, and blending smoothly with personal computing practices. They should allow for convenient movement from one file or function to another and for integration of computerized with nonautomated procedures. The Electronic Library will involve a heterogeneous hardware and software environment that requires a heavy emphasis on compatibility, linking, and interoperability through standardized protocols. The technical complexities of providing such service should be invisible to the library user.

FROM SERVICE TO SELF-SERVICE

The potential use of library service greatly exceeds the actual use, which is known to be sensitive to convenience. On the one hand, use of the Electronic Library depends on a technical infrastructure that is increasingly in place, at least as far as the users of university and corporate library services are concerned. On the other hand, the Electronic Library appears to remove many of the constraints of the Paper Library, such as the effective limitation to local collections, the tendency for desired books to be unavailable, limited opening hours, and, especially, the need to go to the library in order to use it. With these constraints removed or moderated there is the prospect of a dramatic increase in library use.

With so much more service possible in the Electronic Library, expanded use of library service seems likely to depend more and more on facilitating self-service than on ever more one-on-one service by library staff, even though the latter will remain necessary and desirable, and even though the tasks facing library users will become more complex. Funding for a corresponding increase in library staffing seems unlikely. Even if it were provided, an ever increasing proportion of the use of library services will be from outside the library building. A strategic shift from the direct provision of service one-on-one to the design and provision of library services intended for self-service seems inevitable, even though library services are becoming more powerful and more complex.

COPING WITH COMPLEXITY

Where there is increasing complexity, problems arise when the user's expertise is inadequate for the task. Different sorts of response are possible[1]:

1. *User education:* Expertise can be increased.
2. *Advice:* The system could possibly be designed to offer helpful guidance or prompts.
3. *Simplification:* If the complexity facing the user could be reduced, then the user's expertise would become more adequate *relative to* the task.
4. *Mediation:* Providing an expert human intermediary to provide assistance—a reference librarian, for example—is an obvious course of action.
5. *Delegation:* It may be possible to shift some of the task complexity inside the system to make the system itself smarter and more capable of determining what should be done next.

These different responses are not mutually exclusive. Which, or which combination, would be most cost-effective in any given case may vary greatly.

ASSISTANCE

Difficulties arise both because library users' needs are so extensive and so varied and because the sources of information are too complex, too imperfect, and too incomplete for self-service to be adequate. It is inherently unreasonable to assume that the provision of unaided library "self-service" will be satisfactory. Assistance is needed of three overlapping kinds: reference service, library instruction, and referral.

Reference Service

In addition to answering questions on almost every conceivable topic, reference librarians provide assistance on research projects, explain the use of complex bibliographic tools, arrange computerized searches of many different databases, conduct on-line information searches, and (as noted later in this chapter) offer both formal and informal instruction in the use of library services. Some requests can be answered with simple, factual information, but others may take hours or even days of investigation.

The user's first significant task is to identify and locate needed material. For many types of materials, the bibliographic tools available for this task are complex or incomplete, and the user is unlikely to be successful in finding the material needed without help. Librarians are therefore needed to assist users in interpreting such tools, and to ensure that all suitable possible sources of information are made known to the reader.

The advent of computerized services for searching machine-readable databases has also added a new dimension to reference and information services. Many of the major abstracting and indexing services, such as *Chemical Abstracts* and the *Readers' Guide,* are now searched on-line as well as on paper. Increasingly bibliographies are available not only from on-line search services but also as optical digital disks (CD-ROMs) that can be searched inside the library and as files mounted on on-line library catalogs. The commands to use these systems differ, and the on-line version may not be the same as the paper version where both exist.

Library Instruction

There are various ways in which instruction in using libraries can be given. At the simplest level, there is the familiar "orientation" technique, or guided tour, the main purpose of which is to familiarize students with the layout of the library building and the location of various resources and services. At a more specific level, there are also "point-of-use" instructions, including printed guides on basic techniques in using the resources of the library; brochures on how to use bibliographic tools, such as indexing and abstracting services; videotape, audiotape, and slide-tape presentations; and personal guidance by reference librarians in methods of pursuing research in particular fields.

A third type of instruction has also gained increasing support in academic libraries: the formal course in bibliographic and research methods offered for academic credit and particularly designed for undergraduate students. The major objective of such classes is to impart skills for continuing self-education on the part of the student.

Library instruction can be expensive and labor-intensive, but the prospect of a major increase in self-service makes it an important and a plausible investment. Library service can be characterized by reaching out to teach. It is unsatisfactory for all parties for there to be frustrated, unsuccessful users.

Referral

A third form of assistance is referral to other sources. This might be referring a difficult question to another, more specialized library, librarian, or other expert ("reference referral") or referring a library user to another more appropriate source. In both cases it is necessary to know to whom or to where a referral can be made with a reasonable chance of success. The development of detailed knowledge of resources is necessary for referral to work effectively.

Library use and bibliographic research are complex and becoming more so. A greater investment in user education will be needed to ensure that effective use is made of library resources, all the more so as any library's resources come to include the resources of all cooperating libraries. Such an investment is needed if library users are to achieve a substantial benefit from the investment in the creation of future library services.

Note

1. Michael K. Buckland and Doris Florian, "Expertise, Task Complexity, and Artificial Intelligence: A Conceptual Framework," *Journal of the American Society for Information Science* 42 (1991):635–43.

8

Organization and Implementation

ORGANIZATION AND GOVERNANCE

Whatever scheme for service might be designed, implementation is unlikely to be, or to remain, successful unless there is a proper political and economic structure of governance, authority, resource allocation, and accountability. Failure to develop satisfactory governance and organizational structures can have very serious consequences. Nevertheless, for three reasons, this area will not be examined in any detail beyond the noting of a few general guidelines.

First, organizational structures and governance tend to be situational: They need to be compatible with the culture and traditions of the larger organization or community that the library serves. Arrangements that might be acceptable in one situation might not be acceptable in another.

Second, flexibility and adaptability are important. The characteristics of the Automated Library are different enough from those of the Paper Library to indicate changes in organization.[1] The Electronic Library, in turn, will have its own characteristics that can be expected to lead to additional changes in the management and organization of libraries.

Third, organization and governance should, in a sense, be the last aspects to be considered. This assertion is not meant to diminish their importance but is, rather, a tactical consideration. Different organizational structures lend themselves to different sorts of activities. Manufacturing organizations, for example, tend to function differently from service organizations. In manufacturing, differences have been found in the organizational structures suited for small-batch production, for large-batch production, and for continuous-process production. In service activities, differences have been found in organizational structures between routine services and professional services.

For these reasons any existing structure or any specific structure that might be designed will necessarily be more suitable for some activities and circumstances than for others.[2] In this way "organizational technology" shares the attributes of any other technology: Each approach offers different constraints in terms of the activities for which it is suited. Given the importance of compatibility between activities and administrative structure, to start by assuming or prescribing any given organizational structure is to impose the constraints and limitations of that organizational structure from the beginning. It would, ideally, seem better to defer administrative considerations and to concentrate initially on the needs of library users and on the potential of available information technology. After that is accomplished, political and economic realities will have to be considered. By deferring that consideration the desired design for service will have been less inhibited, and there will be a better basis for evolving organizational structures consistent with what one is trying to achieve. That might seem the best course of action in theory, but the show has to go on: Governance and organizational structure cannot be suspended.

The organizational structure of a library tends to be relatively complex because it reflects a mixture of technologies: Technical services resemble continuous-process manufacturing; circulation and shelving are routine-service activities; and reference work is a professional-service activity. A library, then, includes three of the five different types of organizational structure distinguished previously.

For discussion of organization and governance, reference should be made to general management texts.[3] Important guidelines include:

Responsibility should be accompanied by authority and resources.
Authority should be balanced by accountability.
Accountability depends on effective dissemination of information and on mechanisms for decision making.
Any structure needs to be compatible with and acceptable to its parent organization.
Cooperative and exchange arrangements should be mutually beneficial.
Flexibility and the ability to adapt enable an organization to evolve.

IMPLEMENTATION OF CHANGE

Good planning is a process that leads to consistent anticipatory decision making. Planning that does not influence decisions is futile. Decision making should be anticipatory in that plans should be ready as (or before) events occur. Decisions should be consistent with the mission of the organization and with other decisions. Bad planning or, more commonly, an absence of planning is reflected in decisions that are taken too late and that are inconsistent: Any good resulting from one decision is liable to be undone by the next.

A plan in the form of a document is not strictly necessary for good planning since planning can be done in the mind. A written plan is a tool usually designed for a specific purpose: to establish consensus, to generate approval, to communicate, or to obtain resources.

With technological change there is often unfortunate confusion between "research and development" and "innovation." Research and development have to do with the *identification* of feasible new options and is a matter of inquiry, investigation, and testing. Innovation is a matter of selecting or rejecting available options and is a management activity. These are quite different activities. Failure to recognize the difference between them leads to the development of options that are not properly considered or to the adoption of impractical or unsuitable innovations.[4]

The management of research and development, the implementation of change, and effective planning are important and widely underestimated skills. There is a large and useful literature on planning upon which one can draw.[5]

Notes

1. Michael Gorman, "The Ecumenical Library," *The Reference Librarian* 9 (1984):55–64.

2. Richard L. Daft, *Management*, 2d ed. (Chicago: Dryden Press, 1991), Chapter 10.

3. See, for example, Daft, *Management*; Harold Koontz, Cyril O'Donnell, and Heinz Weihrich, *Management*, 8th ed. (New York: McGraw-Hill, 1984).

4. For a review of this and other causes of failure in the move from the Paper Library to the Automated Library, see Stephen R. Salmon, *Library Automation Systems* (New York: Marcel Dekker, 1975), Chapter 9.

5. For a start, see, for example, Harold Koontz, Cyril O'Donnell, and Heinz Weihrich, *Management*, 8th ed. (New York: McGraw-Hill, 1984), Chapters 5 and 10; Stanton F. Biddle, *Planning University Library Services* (New York: Greenwood, [Forthcoming]).

The Challenge

The mission of library service is to support the purposes of the group to be served. The role of library service is to provide access to documents. We could, if we wished, choose to define documents generously to include a range of informative objects that can be stored and retrieved, not only writings and not only published writings.

Library service may be concerned with knowledge, but it is so in a fashion that is doubly indirect. Firstly, library services are concerned with texts and images that are representations of knowledge. Secondly, library services are, in practice, often concerned less with the texts and images themselves than with physical objects that are text-bearing and image-bearing, such as books, journals, manuscripts, and photographs. Libraries deal with text-bearing and image-bearing objects in vast quantities. Much of libraries' operating budgets and space is devoted not to the *use* of these materials, but to *assembling, organizing, and describing* these materials so that it becomes possible to use them. Hence, any significant change in the technology of text-bearing objects or of handling them could have very profound consequences, not on the purpose and mission of library services, but on the means for achieving them.

TECHNOLOGICAL CHANGE

There is overwhelming consensus concerning trends in unit costs in information technology:

the cost of computing power will continue to decrease rapidly, data storage costs will continue to decrease steadily, and the technology of telecommunications indicates strong long-term reductions.

Software, being labor-intensive to develop and maintain, should not be assumed to share in the dramatic improvements in hardware costs. Nevertheless the overall trend is very clear: Computer-based operations are becoming steadily and substantially more affordable. The practical conclusion is easily drawn. To the extent that computer-based procedures *can* be substituted for pre-computer procedures, they will be. Overall, the amount of computer-based activity will increase.

Information technology may only be a means and not an end, but that does not make it unimportant. We have just noted that in the provision of library service a very large proportion of present budgets is devoted to arranging the means to enable service to be provided. The substitution of computing power, electronic data storage, and use of telecommunications holds considerable potential, not least because of the expectation that they will continue to become more attractive on cost grounds. The important questions become how and when the substitution of procedures based on new information technology should be adopted. The constraints include our limited ability to determine how to achieve that substitution, when that substitution will become cost-effective, and, at least as important, how to discriminate between substitutions that support improved library service and substitutions that subvert the mission and role of library service.

BEYOND SUBSTITUTION

The initial task can reasonably be to find out how and when to substitute techniques using new information technology in the place of more traditional methods. This, in itself, misjudges the real options. Each technology offers a different set of constraints. Each technology is suited for doing *different* things. The automating of manual procedures may well be worthwhile, but, in the longer term, misses the point of technological change. The initial question may be: How could library services be advantageously automated? This is a matter of doing the *same* things better. The longer term, more interesting question is: How could library service be redesigned with a change in technology? This is a matter of how to do better, *different* things.

Critical for addressing the second question—which better, different things should be done—is an understanding of past constraints upon library services that are attributable to the constraints of the technology of paper, card, and microform. However, constraints that are familiar tend to be transparent and not easy to recognize.

In Chapter 2, we noted the constraints of paper. Paper is a strictly localized medium; a paper document is generally suited for use by only one person at a time; paper copies of paper documents have the same constraints as do the original; paper records are rather inflexible and can become expensively bulky. These constraints, in turn, determine the major limitations of the library service based on paper and paper-like technology:

1. Only documents that are local are usable. In all other cases the document must be fetched or the user must travel. The contents, scale, and suitability of the *local* collection dominates the quality of library service in the Paper Library and in the Automated Library.

2. Space for storing large local collections can become a significant practical problem.

3. Paper documents can be copied but are otherwise inflexible.

4. Catalogs on card are more flexible (but less movable) than catalogs in printed book form. In both cases adding points of access becomes very cumbersome. Traditional U.S. practice has been to maintain access by author, subject heading, and title. Each requires an additional sequence of cards. Adding sequences to provide access by date, for example, or by language becomes prohibitively expensive. Economical subject access is at the price of using a highly complex pre-coordinate subject-heading system, such as the *Library of Congress Subject Headings*.

5. Users, catalog, documents, and bibliographies are physically separate from each other. There is inconvenience in getting from any one to any other.

6. Paper Libraries are closed much of the time and are invariably at some distance from the user.

7. Sought documents are commonly unavailable because they are already being used (or, more likely, not actually being used but borrowed) by someone else.

8. Time and patience are often needed to use Paper Libraries.

9. The problems of Paper Libraries are sensitive to size. Small libraries are limited in what they can provide. In large libraries there are diseconomies of scale because unit costs of filing, finding, and reshelving increase as collections become larger.

Computer-based processing and electronic document storage have been found to have their own distinctive characteristics. The constraints include a greater need for standardization, increased technical complexity, and greater dependence on equipment that is much more fragile and much more prone to obsolescence than that of a Paper Library.

Advantages of the new technology are that repetitive, mechanical tasks can be delegated to the machinery; the rate of increase in labor costs can thereby be moderated; electronic records can be modified, rearranged, and combined with each other; and, with telecommunications, distance becomes substantially irrelevant. These factors transform those aspects of library service that derive from the constraints of paper and cardboard. The location of the user, the catalog record, the bibliography, and the document cease to be dominating considerations. The user, the catalog, the bibliography, and the document can now be connected in ways that, hitherto, could only be dreamed about. As these changed constraints come to be appreciated, it becomes clear that these new circumstances offer the possibility—indeed the inevitability—of new designs for library service.

Several major changes are indicated:

1. Since library materials in electronic form lend themselves to remote access and shared use, the assembling of local collections becomes less important. Coordinated collection development and cooperative, shared access to collections become more important.

2. With materials on paper, having copies stored locally is a necessary (though not a sufficient) condition for convenient access. With electronic materials, local storage may be desirable but is no longer necessary. Therefore, a catalog defined as a guide to what is locally stored becomes progressively less complete as a guide to what is conveniently accessible. One might as well catalog books published in odd years but not those published in even years. The answer is to shift from catalogs to union catalogs or linked catalogs and to holdings data linked to bibliographies, thus reversing our usual perspective on catalogs as bibliographic descriptions attached to holdings records. Arguably the present-day catalog, on-line or on cards, is more a product of the limitations of nineteenth-century library technology than of present-day opportunities.

3. In the meanwhile, those to be served are changing their information-handling habits. Paper and pen are being supplemented by desktop workstations capable of using a multiplicity of remote sources. This leads to an entirely different perspective: from a library-centered world view to one that is user-centered.

4. These technological changes also invite reconsideration of the professional orthodoxy of consolidating academic library services. The view that a multiplicity of branch and departmental libraries is inefficient might well change. Under different conditions the decentralization of library service might well be regarded as an effective strategy by administrators as well by as users.

5. The trend is to digitize everything for storage and manipulation: sound, image, moving images, text, and numeric data. Documents of all

kinds are becoming more homogeneous in their physical medium. Limiting libraries to printed documents, or, indeed, written documents, makes less and less sense. If that demarcation dissolves, there is a blurring of boundaries. The function of the library, the computer center, and the telecommunications office are converging, overlapping, or, at least, more closely related. New patterns are evolving in the relationships between libraries, publishers, and the information industry. The roles of archives, libraries, museums, and other information stores seem likely to become less clearly differentiated.

6. There is much greater opportunity to bring service to wherever potential users of library service happen to be.

Catalogs, collections, buildings, and library staff are the familiar means for providing library services. Computers, networks, and electronic documents provide additional means with interesting possibilities.

Hitherto library services have been dominated by local catalogs, local collections, and great inequalities in the geographical distribution of services. The constraints on library service are changing right now. None of this is an argument for abandoning paper and local collections. All of this requires us to think again about the mission of the library, the role of the library, and the means of providing service. For the first time in one hundred years we face the grand and difficult challenge of redesigning library services.

Appendix

SOURCES

The best way to explore these issues is talking with others with similar interests. This is now facilitated by several electronic bulletin boards and "listservers" (e.g., PACS-L@UHUPVM.BITNET and CNIDIR-L @UNMVM.BITNET) through which one can engage in dialogue with those active in the field. Conferences organized by, for example, the American Library Association and its divisions, the American Society for Information Science, and EDUCOM are likely to be helpful.

A convenient short specialized guide to resources with an emphasis on university libraries can be found in Arms, Carolyn A., ed., *Campus Strategies for Libraries and Electronic Information,* pp. 373–81. N.p.: Digital Press, 1990. There is also a glossary and accounts of developments in selected U.S. university libraries.

More generally, a systematic approach to published literature is not very practical because little of what is published addresses in any direct way the sorts of strategic issues examined in this book and because what is published is not concentrated in any one place. It may occur in general publications such as *American Libraries* or the *Journal of Documentation* or in specialized journals such as *Cataloging and Classification Quarterly* or *College and Research Libraries.* Technology-oriented journals, such as *Information Technology and Libraries* and *Library Hi Tech,* also carry material on longer term issues but are, for the most part, concerned with shorter term, more technical matters.

In library catalogs using Library of Congress Subject Headings try the subject headings "Library Science—Forecasting" and "Information Science—Forecasting."

There are, of course, the usual sources on library services:

Bibliographies

Library & Information Science Abstracts. London: Library Association, 1969– .
Library Hi Tech Bibliography. Ann Arbor, Mich.: Pierian Press, 1986– .
Library Literature. New York: H. W. Wilson Co., 1934– .

Reviews

Advances in Librarianship. New York: Academic Press, 1970– .
Advances in Library Administration and Organization. Greenwich, Conn.: JAI Press, 1982– .
ALA Yearbook of Library and Information Services. Chicago: American Library Association, 1984– .
Annual Review of Information Science and Technology. New York: Interscience Publishers, 1966– .
Library Trends. Urbana, Ill.: University of Illinois, Graduate School of Library and Information Science, 1952– .

Specialized Journals

Educom Review. Washington, D.C.: Educom, 1966– .
Information Technology and Libraries. Chicago: Library and Information Technology Association, 1982– .
Library Hi Tech. Ann Arbor, Mich.: Pierian Press, 1983– .

Works likely to be useful for background material and bibliographies include:

Baker, Sharon L., and F. W. Lancaster, *Measurement and Evaluation of Library Services.* 2nd ed. Arlington, Va.: Information Resources Press, 1991.

Shuman, Bruce A. *The Library of the Future: Alternative Scenarios for the Information Profession.* Englewood, Colo.: Libraries Unlimited, 1989. A good brief introduction to future studies, with alternative scenarios for U.S. public library development.

SPEC Kits issued by the Systems and Procedures Center of the Office of Management Studies of the Association of Research Libraries, Washington, D.C.

Taylor, Robert S. *Value-Added Processes in Information Systems*. Norwood, N.J.: Ablex, 1986.

Vickery, Brian C., and Alina Vickery. *Information Science in Theory and Practice*. London: Butterworths, 1987.

Index

Michael Buckland is Professor of Library and Information Studies, University of California, Berkeley. He studied at Oxford and Sheffield universities and worked as a librarian in England and in the USA. Professor Buckland has been Dean of the School of Library and Information Studies at Berkeley and Vice President for Library Plans and Policies in the University of California system-wide administration. His writings include *Book Availability and the Library User* (Pergamon, 1975), *Information and Information Systems* (Praeger, 1991), and *Library Services in Theory and Context* (2d ed, Pergamon, 1988).